Talitha Koum
LITTLE GIRL, RISE!

REBEKAH MARQUEZ

WESTBOW
PRESS®
A DIVISION OF THOMAS NELSON
& ZONDERVAN

WestBow Press books may be ordered through booksellers or by contacting:

WestBow Press
A Division of Thomas Nelson & Zondervan
1663 Liberty Drive
Bloomington, IN 47403
www.westbowpress.com
1 (866) 928-1240

Because of the dynamic nature of the Internet, any web addresses or links contained in this book may have changed since publication and may no longer be valid. The views expressed in this work are solely those of the author and do not necessarily reflect the views of the publisher, and the publisher hereby disclaims any responsibility for them.

This book is a work of non-fiction. Unless otherwise noted, the author and the publisher make no explicit guarantees as to the accuracy of the information contained in this book and in some cases, names of people and places have been altered to protect their privacy.

Any people depicted in stock imagery provided by Thinkstock are models, and such images are being used for illustrative purposes only. Certain stock imagery © Thinkstock.

ISBN: 978-1-5127-8341-4 (sc)
ISBN: 978-1-5127-8343-8 (hc)
ISBN: 978-1-5127-8342-1 (e)

Library of Congress Control Number: 2018901019

Print information available on the last page.

WestBow Press rev. date: 05/29/2018

I want to thank those who stood by me while I battled through the process of writing this book. Without women praying for me and with me, I wouldn't have written a word. I thank God for the power of prayer and the wisdom of faith. I especially want to thank my family for their encouragement. Their courage and support is a testament to God's forgiveness and His gift of redemption in my life.

I'd stay in the garden with Him
Though the night around me be falling.
But He bids me go; through the voice of woe
His voice to me is calling.

—Charles A. Miles, "The Garden"

Contents

Introduction

In the beginning, I didn't want to write this book. I didn't want people to see what I've been hiding for so many years. Secrets that not even my daughters knew. Hidden places never exposed to light for fear that the light might expose too much, and I'd be crushed by its truth. But God.

I've been on this journey for a few years now. Every day I pray, "God, lead me to where You want me to go." I've received counsel from people I know are anointed with Father's love. However, at times, life's noises seemed so loud that all I could hear was its distractions. It was during one of those distracting times that I felt His call to write. All I could say was, "Really, God. *Now?*"

I would like to say that I took a holy approach and just started to write. But no. Not quite. I've been writing for years and had stopped for a period of my life. Life's busyness often doesn't allow that creative side to flow, so I put it aside. Now, at a time in my life while unemployed and with chaos at home, He decides that I should start. But God doesn't stop there. He tells me that He wants me to write about my life. As I prayed and listened, all I could do was weep and ask, "Why?" I am no different from a lot of people who have struggled and continue to struggle with a childhood that was not of His design. God did not design children to be abused, molested, ignored, and made to feel worthless. He created His children to be loved and treasured, but many who have been abused don't understand that truth. So why ask me? Really? It's just me. Rebekah. A nobody. Well, I would like to say that He gave me a great revelation, but all He said was, "Write." It took a few years of soul searching and prayer. Especially when He told me the subject matter. My life is not a place that I've wanted to dive into many times, but He made it very clear that's where He wanted to start.

While going through a healing journey the revelation became clearer. Sitting in a circle with about seven other women, I began telling my story. I had a little trouble at first, as this was all new to me. As I read aloud what I had written, it hit me: this was my first time telling my story, and it sounded disheartening. I never understood the importance of telling secrets that weren't meant to stay in dark places. They festered and perverted the core of who I was meant to be. For a year I had asked God to change my DNA into His DNA. I wanted Him to change me back into the person I was meant to be before all the junk others had laid on me. It's funny how He answers prayers. His way is never our way but it's always better.

A few weeks after my encounter with the Journey group, God began speaking to me. He said that He wanted me to write. Not just for a group, but for more eyes to see. *Yikes!*—that's an understatement of what was going through my mind. So God and I began this journey, but it all began in prayer.

After the group was completed and while I was going through some really difficult places, He continued to insist, "Write." The battle in my home was making my heart feel worthless and broken again. I asked God, "Why are you allowing this in my life again if you want me to write?" I have found that sometimes He doesn't answer but continues to point to our destiny. "Write," is all He would say.

One morning as I sat praying and weeping for my current struggle, I saw a vision of me going into an attic. A small light appeared in the attic, and as I looked around, all I saw were boxes made out of wood. There weren't many, but they all would require a crowbar to open. Suddenly I heard *bang, bang, bang, bang!* I noticed that the banging was coming from a door in front of me. In my spirit, I knew that the demons from my past where trying to come back. Bang, bang, bang! The noise was so loud that I couldn't think, and the boxes seemed to become larger and overwhelmed my thoughts. *Bang, bang, bang, bang, bang, bang-bang-bang-bang!* I could feel old fears trying to return. Demons from past hurts were at the door, and they wanted back what was once theirs. Then I noticed the light. It came from a single window above my head and shined directly on the door.

As I focused on the door, I saw Him. I knew His presence. It felt familiar and safe. He said, "Focus on Me. They can't come through. They no longer have any power. Open the boxes and reveal their contents. My power to set people free are in these boxes. Through them you will find who I created you to be. Open and show everyone why you are Mine." His love was so strong that all I could do was cry. So I began writing, with crowbar in hand, opening boxes of my past and exposing their contents to those willing to read. That's a double *yikes*!

Parts of my story are very clear for me, while other parts seem shrouded in darkness and seem scary. But God. If He requires it then there must be a purpose. I have to allow Him and trust Him as He unveils that shroud of darkness, even in the midst of fear. Part of my fear is that I never wanted to dishonor my parents. Although they may have failed, in some way they also gave me the greatest gift—knowing Christ. I knew Him early enough in my life that He personally came to save me. And what good would it do to dishonor people who were broken themselves? They wanted and needed God, but they didn't understand His power—but can any of us say we totally understand His power? It is in the process of letting everything go and becoming spiritually naked before Him that we will find Him. For many of us, that's too difficult. We become hoarders of brokenness piled high, saving hurts that should be thrown away. But we are unable to see beyond our broken mess and actually become secure in its chaos. Then we walk around believing that no one else can see our mess—but believe me, they do. Thank God that He helped me face some of my own junk. He brought wonderful counselors and people who were willing to hear with ears tuned into Father's heart. Because of them I now can face the most difficult hurts and write about it.

My parents thought religious legalism would fix them, devoid of God's power. They believed in healing and in His supernatural power, but they thought that perfection was necessary for the latter. I tried to continue that lie in my own life. I lived with the constant need to do things perfectly. I believed perfection was God's direction since this was my father and mother's confession over me. If I wasn't perfect enough, God wouldn't love me. Although I knew this was a lie, I still believed it. I know that sounds crazy, but only God's power can break a strong curse infused with lies. Through my story, I want to convey how darkness came against me but more importantly how God's love continuously pursued me and saved me. He came to me at times when things were at their worst. The enemy wanted to destroy my brothers and me. Darkness loves to pick on little children. It is the worst bully on the playground and it holds nothing back. If the enemy can break your spirit when you're young, then it can destroy your adult life and nullify God's destiny. Darkness will try to convince you that you are less than what God created you to be. Division will come into your mind and even into your family and can filter through generations. But God—He is the Healer. Nothing is impossible for Him. "He will turn the hearts of the fathers back to the children and turn the hearts of the children back to their fathers" (Malachi 4:6 NIV). This is my prayer as my story unfolds: that Father will direct you back to His embrace and away from darkness; that you will find your own secret place again and in that place, find the courage to break the oppression that has held you back. Go in confidence because God will provide all the healing that you need and in the process, will help you reach your destiny. Amen.

CHAPTER 1

The Power of Father's Hands

And He took the Children in His arms, placed
His hands on them and blessed them.

—Mark 10:16

My father's heart suffered from anemia and it affected his
hands. The disease came from having little and getting less,
so when he smacked me for the first time, the disease had taken
root and was firmly planted deep in his heart. Hands that should
have protected me and rescued me instead pushed me into dark
places. He was familiar with these places. His own introduction
had come from his father's hands and its familiarity made it easy
for my father to convey.

My father was born in 1938 towards the end of the Great
Depression. In Puerto Rico, the Great Depression was their daily
existence, so this tide only enhanced what they already didn't
have. Living in a one-room shack with no running water or
electricity was my father's family's lot in life and hopelessness was
their cloak. Growing up with four brothers and a sister under a
tin roof and wooden walls was their natural reality. My father and
his brothers were required to bring water from the river; carried

in jugs on their heads. His mother cooked for a family of seven using three large stones heated over a fire, absent of the modern conveniences of knobs and gauges. My father never wore shoes until the age of fourteen. By that time his feet had become as callused as his heart.

My grandfather was short in stature, but he ruled his family with controlled authority. At times his authority came with little mercy, especially after hurting his back, causing him to lose his job. As the realization of his failure manifested, he began drinking which ignited his anger and rage. Feeding the family and being a provider was a man's job. That wasn't more true anywhere than in his Latin culture. My grandfather became a bitter man and he often took out his frustration on his family, especially my father. In his drunken state, he would brutally whip my father, which left scars on his back. Love was doled out as scarcely as food, so when it was shown, the children received it with bloated bellies and starved hearts.

One Christmas, when my father was about eight years old, his older brother told him that their father had bought him a cowboy shirt. My father loved anything to do with cowboys. Many times he would run away from his father's beatings and sneak into the small theater in town and watch John Wayne movies. He dreamed of going to the United States and riding a horse off into the sunset. The night before this great gift was to be given, he stayed up all night in anticipation. He felt special, not just because of the gift but also because of the giver. He knew that his father had very little, yet he was lavishing him with a personal and loving gift. To this day, the thought of this gift brings my father to tears. When morning finally arrived and they were able to open their gifts, my father danced at the sight of his yellow cowboy shirt trimmed with maroon thread and a stitching of a cowboy on its shoulder. Immediately he put on his shirt, rarely taking it off. It was a sad day when the threadbare shirt became too small for him to wear.

So when he became a father, he ruled his home with authority, but it was warped by years of his abuse and lack of love, wrapped in the memory of a shirt that had long faded.

We lived in New Jersey in the projects called Grant Street Apartments when his hands first introduced me into his darkness. We were surrounded by large, ominous buildings made of brick and mortar. Nothing about the buildings was warm. They were simply places to house people, like chickens in a coop. I didn't fear the area but the memories seem cold and distant. The apartment we lived in was small with white walls and industrial tiles, waxed and shined by my mother to a sparkling white. Walking in, the first thing you'd see was the open dining and living room area. To the right of the entrance was a galley kitchen with a large white porcelain sink. To the left was a short dark hallway, with three doors leading to two bedrooms and a bathroom.

My parents had a crib in their room for me, but soon I would be displaced because my mother was pregnant. I didn't understand the concept, so I didn't care about the event. I just knew that they were getting ready for someone new and I was excited for the interruption. Every day my mother tackled the small apartment as if dirt and dust were a personal affront to her. My mother's spotless home would make visitors take off their shoes as if entering holy ground covered in wax. When guests came for dinner, if they dropped any food they would instantly retrieve it and eat as if they were eating from their own plates. In their minds, the floor was as clean as their plates, so the act came naturally.

Our favorite visitor was our aunt Maria, my mother's sister. Whenever she entered, the rhythm of her steps made her thick dark curls bounce, and her coffee-colored skin glistened with exuberance. She didn't come often, but my brother and I loved when she came to see us. One Saturday as she entered the dining area, we ran to her, screaming, "Titi! Titi!" ("Auntie" in Spanish). She always brought us gifts and with them lots of hugs and kisses, something we lacked in our home. My mother was constantly doing and my father was constantly going, so they rarely spent quality time with us. My aunt was still young and single, so she could afford the luxury of giving affection without the worry of not having enough for herself. She hugged us while speaking to my parents, especially to my mom. "So what did you do for little Rebekah's birthday? I didn't hear anything from you."

At that, both of my parents turned red. "I guess we forgot. We've been very involved with church and the new baby," my mother said.

My aunt gave them a look of disbelief but covered it with a smile. In her hand she had a gift for me, so she handed it to me while speaking to my parents. "Well, let's give her a birthday party today." It was Saturday and they had no excuses. During the week my dad was working, and my mom was at home, cleaning. Sundays were in church for most of the day, so Saturday was the only day left for a party. A month of forgetfulness breeds a lot of guilt, so they gave in to her wish and my mother went to the kitchen to start on the cake. They were very religious Christians and parties weren't part of their holy equation. As a matter of fact, God was my father's best friend and he made sure we all knew it. The man was the head of the household and what he said was always backed by God—at least according to my father. Parties weren't a part of my father's godly rules and were rarely done. As for me, I was two years old and it didn't matter but my aunt persisted and my parents relented.

My gift from my titi was a pink dress that she insisted I wear. She took me to my parents' room and dressed me. She laughed at my silly worm dance as I got out of my clothing. When she put on the pink tulle dress, it expanded at the waist with such confidence that I instantly felt prettier. My dress could make any ballerina jealous with its massive fluffy bottom that bounced when I walked. She helped me put on white socks trimmed in lace fringes and then my best churchgoing shiny black patent leather Mary Jane's. My hair was naturally curly and wild, but she tamed my curls into Shirley Temple ringlets.

Meanwhile, she kept telling me, "Mama, you look so beautiful." Calling me *Mama* was her Latin way of calling me sweetheart or honey. Her voice would rise at "beautiful" and her eyes would light up so for that moment I felt the truth of her words. My eyelashes were long and curly and she was so enamored by them that she decided to put mascara on them. She pulled a tube out of her purse. Secretively, she whispered while applying the mascara, "Shhh, Mama, don't tell anyone." She smiled as she pulled back a few inches and said, "Awww, you look so beautiful."

I knew that makeup was bad, at least, according to my dad. I started feeling a little anxious and my tummy started acting funny. Maybe it was the excitement of the moment or the knowledge that I was doing something bad, or the fact that the dress itched, but I began to worry. I didn't know how to express myself to my aunt, who loved me so much that I felt its warmth down to the core of my heart. I knew my parents loved me, even if they didn't or couldn't always show it. But my aunt's love made me feel special and unique, so I stood quietly and tried my best not to worry about my sticky eyelashes and itchy dress.

Finally and with great bravado, my aunt took me to the dining room where my mom had a cake ready for me. I could see the white tablecloth and the pink cake in the middle. My mother's face brightened when she saw me. My aunt paraded me in front of my father as he sat on our green sofa, watching television. He smiled but seemed annoyed at the whole celebratory atmosphere. My aunt tried to convince my father to join us, but after a few minutes she gave up. My mom took me by the hand and lifted me onto a chair, where I stood as they sang "Happy Birthday." My mom's soprano voice was beautiful. My father neither joined us nor turned to sing. I became convinced that my father didn't join us because of my secret. My two-year-old mind didn't understand that my secret wasn't really bad, so I began to cry, believing that I had upset my father. The sight of black streaks running down my face made my aunt and mom nervous. My mom gave my aunt a dirty look and my aunt tried her best not to laugh at the sight of me. They tried to pacify me but instead created louder cries and more tears. I saw my dad turn around and look at me. In a moment, he was coming at me with the force of a bull that had seen red, but rage wasn't something I understood. I raised my arms in innocent surrender, believing that my father was coming to rescue me. I closed my eyes and cried louder. I felt a sting across my face and lost my balance off the chair. Anyone looking in would have thought that a little fairy had lost her wings and was landing with a crash. I landed in the corner of the room, a puddle of small limbs, pink tulle, and raccoon eyes. My crying was reduced to a few hiccups. I heard yelling and screaming and felt someone pick me up. I was taken into my parents' room and put in the crib.

Alone, I lay my head down. Tears streamed down my face, mixed with a silent sob. I could hear fighting and banging outside my door, but my mind didn't understand. I barely understood what had just happened to me. I could feel the sting on my face as a warm sensation throbbed and swelled my cheek. Then the realization of what had happened started to form in my small mind as I touched the place that was still heated by my father's anger. My father had hit me. Without much understanding, my spirit heard a quiet break in the middle of my chest. That day a small fissure began, too small for the human eye to see but big enough for darkness to slip in. A part of who I was died at that moment, and my father's numbness began to take its place. God made me beautiful, loving, and trusting. Some of that had been broken, and with it came a lot of sadness.

Then He came to me. He reached down, touching the place where my father had hit me. His hands were cool, and I felt His compassion, His grief, His brokenness, and His deep love for me. I closed my eyes and reached my little hand between the railings to Him. At His touch, I was outside the crib, standing next to Him. I found myself walking away with Him. At that moment I didn't know where we were going, but I knew it was better than where I was now. Somehow, my spirit knew Him and wanted to be with

Him. I left "Little Girl Me" in her crib by herself. I looked back at her. Her eyes were closed with black tears slowly coming down her face. Quiet sobs would escape her lips but were muffled by the two fingers she was sucking on. I felt sad for Little Girl Me, but I was too young to understand and I couldn't stay. So I turned, grabbed His hand, and went with my Father to our secret place.

CHAPTER 2

Who's Afraid of the Big Bad Wolf?

Be alert and of sober mind. Your enemy
the devil prowls around ...
Looking for someone to devour.

—1 Peter 5:8

What startled us was the sudden banging. My father was
cursing at my mother in Spanish and yelling, "Open the
door!" Within moments, my father knocked down the door and
ran into the apartment. Knocking furniture out of his way, he
attempted to get to my mother and her new friend. It had been
peaceful, and laughter had filled our new apartment moments
before my father broke in. Peace is the first thing to leave when the
wolf breaks down the door.

My mother was born in Puerto Rico. By the time she was ten
years old, her father had deserted the family—my mother, her three
brothers and sister, and their mother—for another woman. Although
he lived within walking distance in a large home, he rarely came to

see them. My *abuela* (grandma) would walk to his home dragging my mom along, and beg him for food to feed his children. Most times he would send them away empty-handed, or he would give them oranges from his backyard and tell my abuela, "You can't eat any of these." While in Puerto Rico, all six of them lived in a one-room efficiency apartment.

At some point my abuela left Puerto Rico for New York City. She wanted to give her children a better life and knew that staying wasn't an option. She flew into New York City and began to work at a factory. Meanwhile, her children stayed with her sister in Puerto Rico. My abuela sent money back to her sister for my mom and her siblings. When she had enough money, she sent for them. Once again they lived in a one-room efficiency but now in New York City. My mother, being the oldest, was taken out of school to help her mother when she began working two jobs. Resentment started taking root in my mother's heart. She enjoyed school but because of her home environment, she wasn't allowed to finish. By the time she married my dad, she had been cooking and cleaning for her siblings. Maybe marriage seemed a good trade off for her. How could she have known what that trade would entail? Her heart had already been compromised by years of neglect and lack of a father's love.

At the time my father broke into our new apartment, my mother was separated from him. She couldn't take anymore of my father's beatings and belittling words. He often would beat her with his fist and rarely spoke kindness to her. He treated her as if she was his slave and in a depressing way she was. Once they were separated, she introduced us to her new friend. She never had brought a friend home before, so we found ourselves trying our best to entertain him. My father, however, somehow found out about our visitor and kicked down the door with a huff and a puff. His eyes looked wild and his breathing was loud and erratic. His rage was raw; nothing about him looked like my father. His dark curly hair had lost its place and seemed possessed. My mother and her friend ran into her bedroom and locked themselves in. My brothers hid under their bed. My father's madness ran past me. I feared he would hit me so I opened a closet door and let its darkness hide me. He was wild with anger, and I could hear his breathing as he ran down the narrow hallway like an animal after its prey. With a loud boom he knocked the door down and they were trapped. We lived high up in the projects, so there wasn't anywhere for them to go without jumping to their deaths. Like trapped animals, they waited for the great beast to devour them and he did. My father began beating the man and yelling obscenities in Spanish. My mother screamed for him to stop. My father was gone and in his place was a wolf ready to devour anything in his path. As I heard the commotion, my four-year-old curiosity took hold. I couldn't stop my trembling legs from walking toward the door. I peeked through the sliver of an opening and saw my father beating the man. The man fought until he became free. He ran down the hallway, through the dining room and out the front door. My father didn't follow him. His focus was already on my mother. She screamed my father's name and asked him not to hit her. My poor mother; she had already gotten so many blows from my father. His past beatings would knock her out, leaving her senseless on the floor. He often would tell her how unworthy she was and proved it by flagrantly flirting with younger women. How many were her heartaches? Now, she knew what was coming and she knew that this time would be the worst. I could see her body trembling so violently that she could barely stand. Her tears flowed streams of pain already wept too many times. His rage was fast and relentless. He beat her like a man, fist to face, and no matter how she covered herself, he would not stop. I could feel my own fear for my mother rise, and I began to scream. *"Stop!"* That was all I could say, being possessed for a moment by the same demon my father had come in with. Every fiber of my little body shook and I wanted to kill my father. For a split second he stopped hitting her, turned and looked at me. His eyes were empty. In their place was a thing full of rage, hate and lust for revenge. In those few moments, my mother was able to escape past me, but her legs didn't take her far. My father caught up to her by the bathroom door and pushed her in. She was five steps away from the front door. Five steps away from freedom of what came next. He locked the door behind him, and the sounds that came next were worse than the ones from the bedroom. My mother's screams stopped, replaced by whispers of begging for mercy, mixed with the sound of my father beating her body. Thump, thump, thump. There are no words to describe these sounds. Finally, she stopped crying, but his beating continued. I stood in the hallway, staring at the closed bathroom door, shaking in fear and anger. But four-year-old arms are too short and fists too small to fight wolves.

Unbeknownst to me, my grandmother had come in through the door that was left wide open by my mom's friend. While I was standing in the hallway, she passed me and went into my brother's room. All I remember next was her grabbing me and carting me out the door toward the elevator. But I got loose and ran back into the apartment. The door to the bathroom was now open, so I ran as quickly as I could to find my mother. I stopped in the middle of our small bathroom. It had white tile walls, a white claw-foot tub and a white pedestal sink with black-and-white floor tiles. As I looked around, I saw streaks of blood on the once pure-white tiles. There were handprints where my mother must have tried to stand. A metallic odor was everywhere. My mind panicked. All I wanted to do was find her, and I did. Lying between the toilet and sink, I found her body, dead, lying in pools of blood. Her stillness assured me she was gone. Thoughts of her smiling at me as she bathed me in our white kitchen sink consumed my mind like floodlights in a dark room, hard to see but easy to find. But now she was dead, and the thought of that left me little room to breathe.

I don't remember how long I stood there or who grabbed me, but somehow I found myself in my grandmother's car. My baby brother, who was two years old at the time, was sitting beside me crying. He kept saying, "Mommy, Mommy, I want Mommy." His tears streaked his face, leaving behind sadness and confusion. Sitting next to him,

I put my arms around him, tearless. I knew she was dead, but how could a four-year-old explain that to a two-year-old when she didn't understand it herself? I felt the familiar crack. Broken, my little heart had seen too much; it was too much for me to bear. Not a tear flowed down my face while my brothers cried. The sound filled the car and my head. Darkness came for me. It crept its way into the small cracks in my heart made larger by years of abuse.

I closed my eyes. I felt His presence and knew He was near me. I let go, slow and easy. Years of practice had taught me well. I took His hand and left with Him. I could see my brothers and hear them crying. I could see my grandmother looking ahead as she drove. Were the tears in her eyes for her dead daughter? I didn't care. He was here and I wanted to go. As I left I could see Little Girl Me sitting and staring ahead at nothing, but I didn't feel anything for her. He had come to save me and I wanted—no, I needed—to leave. The numbness was at work in my heart and I wanted to get away. As I left, I took one more look at myself sitting next to my brother. That's when I saw them—my little feet. My short legs stuck straight out allowing me to see the bottoms of my small feet. What was the dried red dust that covered them?

I felt Him tugging my hand as if He knew what I was looking at; as if He knew this would be too much. I turned and walked away, not wanting to understand or to remember. In our secret place, I knew I wouldn't have to do either.

CHAPTER 3

Living with God, Jesus, Holy Ghost, Grandma, and Me

Whoever believes in Him shall not perish
but have eternal life.

—John 3:16

Living with my abuela was like living in a small piece of heaven while still being able to feel hell. I knew that my mother had died. I knew that my father had done it. But I also knew that there was nothing I could do to change it, so I accepted what I couldn't change.

I enjoyed living with my abuela. She loved God more than anyone I had ever known. Of course, I was only about five years old, but to me she seemed to call on Him all the time and I never had experienced that in my parents' home. My father never called on God in front of us. He just seemed to know what God was thinking. My mother was too busy doing, so I never saw or heard her call on God either. But my abuela prayed every day in the silence of her room. I could hear her calling out to Him while she wept. She was strict and religious, like my parents, but she was also relational.

Her religious ideals showed up in her dress and choice of expressions. She never wore pants, makeup, or jewelry (except her wedding ring), and she never danced or listened to "worldly" music. She often spoke of the Holy Ghost and that would just scare the "bad" out of me. *Who wants to be invaded by a ghost?* I thought. She wore her hair in two buns, one in the front to give her hair height and another in the back in a French twist. There were times when I would walk in on her while she was doing her hair. She looked like a troll doll with her kinky hair sticking straight up. It was amazing to see how beautiful her hair looked when she was done, but it always made her look stern. The relational side came out in how she lived her life in total surrender to Him.

My favorite pastime was being in my abuela's galley kitchen, sitting at her small table. It was white and red on top with chrome sides. The chairs were red pleather with chrome legs. From that place, I would watch my abuela create delicious works of art. She was an extraordinary cook. Everything she made was homemade, and she cooked with passion. Our time in the kitchen was full of her smiles and my laughter. She would sing her Spanish gospel songs, and I would hum along. I loved when she would praise God while she chopped, mixed and sprinkled spices, raising her hands and thanking Him for all she had, including me. Sometimes when she would begin to cry, I didn't know if it was because of the onions or because of Him, but it never frightened me. Somehow I sensed His presence and would close my eyes with her to receive Him.

My grandmother's other talent was being an extraordinary seamstress. She could make me any kind of dress, no matter how complicated. But what was more amazing was how she could reupholster furniture. She could rip apart any sofa and make it look brand new, or she would wrap a sofa in plastic, tailored perfectly to every contour. Nothing was impossible for her when she sat behind her sewing machine. That is how she kept food on our table and a roof over our heads. My abuela was a savvy businesswoman. She had her own shop at the top of the hill just blocks away from her apartment. Her shop consisted of four sewing machines and roll upon roll of fabric and plastic. It seemed like every time I went on a call with her, the customer wanted plastic covers. I thought she had invented plastic sofa covers. To this day when I smell the scent of plastic or baby powder (which she applied to the plastic when she was fitting them), my thoughts immediately find their way to her. Her shop was a mess, but she knew where everything was. How I miss seeing her, sewing away on her Singer machines. The machines were black with the word Singer written on the side in gold. *Zzzzzz, zzzzzz*—that was the sound those industrial machines made. She seemed to go on forever; at least that's what it felt like to a five or six-year-old like me.

By the end of the day, her hair would be in full rebellion, coming out the sides of her buns. Her eyes would be red and tired and blinking seemingly on their own. She seemed to work nonstop. If it was Tuesday, it was *Dia de las Damas* (women's ministry day), which meant the women were in charge of the church service. These women would dress in all white and do everything that men would do on Sunday service, except it was Tuesday. It was beautiful to watch them praising God together in white. Some, like my abuela, looked like angels, especially when they would unite in the front of the church and sing together. Their love for Father spilled through the congregation and made even grown men cry.

On one paticular Tuesday, my grandma started getting ready for church. She was so tired that she forgot a vital part of her white uniform. She was running a little late, so she rushed to her room and yelled at me, "Hurry up and get ready!" I dressed and came into the dining room, which was nearest to the front door, and waited for her. Like a white tornado she showed up in the dinning room, yelling, "Hurry! Let's go." As she opened the door, I noticed what she had forgotten. I yelled at her, "Abuela! You forgot!" But she yelled at me, "Hurry up!" She was out the door in one swift motion, leaving me behind.

I continued trying to get her attention, but before I knew it, she was gone as the door started to swing shut. New York apartment doors are very heavy, and they shut pretty quickly, so I ran past the closing door, towards her, as quickly as I could. Running out, I could see her turn the corner toward the elevator. I continued to run down the hall and make the turn toward the elevator, but she was already there. Then the door to the elevator opened wide. There were people inside the elevator, and their eyes opened wide when they saw my abuela. She was looking at me, yelling, "Come on! Get in." She was irritated by my hesitance.

She turned to walk into the elevator and noticed everyone staring at her. While standing over the crack where the elevator meets the floor, she felt the breeze and looked down. To me, as I looked at her, she seemed to go in slow motion. There, with every eye on her, she realized what I had been trying to tell her; she'd forgotten her skirt. There she stood in her white blouse and white slip, holding on to the elevator door. In that moment her face turned red, and she released the door and started running back down the hall, yelling, "Why didn't you tell me?"

That day I found out that Grandma was in great shape. Her white size eight shoes were moving so fast that I could barely keep up. Running behind her all I could say was, "Abuela, I was trying to tell you, but you wouldn't let me." My poor abuela; she was often so tired that these occurrences happened more times than I can tell. Once, she forgot to finish brushing her hair and walked out with her hair sticking straight up. Another time, she was rushing and I was yelling, but the elevator people always got the last word.

My aunt lived with us but stayed out with her boyfriend and her cousins a lot. My abuela's husband lived there too, but he wasn't into kids or church, so I wasn't around him much. I shared the room I slept in with my aunt. We had a window that faced Yankee Stadium. During baseball season, I could hear and see the games. This would often be my form of entertainment when I was bored. There was no television in my grandmother's house. Like many Pentecostals in her time, she believed that evil spirits could be transferred through the television, so I played alone and learned to read books at a young age.

Nothing about living with Abuela was ordinary. We went to the shop every day and came home to her cooking and getting ready and going to church. She was always involved with prayer meetings, women's groups and worship services or with her business. I don't think she believed in slowing down. Sadly, her life was marred by struggles and heartaches.

My grandmother had three sons and they were all lost in the world of addiction. While they were growing up, she worked long hours, sometimes working two jobs. Although my mother was supposed to watch over them, she was their sister and had little authority over them. After moving to New York City, they got involved with friends who introduced them to a life of drugs. This life took them out of her home at an early age. My grandma could often be heard crying in her room, while calling on Father for her children. As she said their names, she would weep uncontrollably and at times I couldn't understand what she was saying. Starting on her knees, she would often end up on her face on the floor. I could feel her pain and anguish coming through. At times I would cry with her. Her last hope was my aunt, who lived with us and was dating a young man in the air force. At times he would come over with my aunt. He liked buying my grandmother gifts from around the world. Once he brought her two Chinese dolls encased in glass. They were beautiful with their white porcelain faces and colorful kimonos. They stood about two feet high. I loved looking at these figures and making up stories about them. Abuela proudly displayed her beautiful ladies in the living room and showed them to everyone who came over. But one day, these ladies came crashing down.

My grandmother had discovered something about my aunt and her boyfriend. I was never told what it was. Assuming that I was too young, I never asked. I had never seen Abuela like this. Through tears and intense anger, she picked up those beautiful dolls encased in their false security and smashed them to the floor. Glass and doll parts splattered across the living floor while my abuela cried. She broke down and collapsed to her knees on the floor. She landed on the only spot in the living room that didn't have broken glass. Her cry was deep. My aunt was the last one left in her home—the last one, and all Abuela's hopes hung on her. Whatever had transpired had left Abuela as broken as the dolls shattered across the floor.

I went into our room and sat on our bed. I shook from the inside out and wondered when was it coming. I could feel a change coming for me, I thought to myself, *"It won't be good."*

My aunt eventually came back and asked Abuela for forgiveness, but something inside of me had shifted. Now I knew that bad things could happen to me, even here. In the next few months, I started school, and with it started the bad things.

CHAPTER 4

Chinese Dolls Go to Heaven

Permit the children to come to Me:
do not hinder them; for the kingdom of
God belongs to such as these.
—Mark 10:14

I loved looking at those Chinese dolls encased in their beautiful glass cocoons. They were propped tall and elegantly. Looking at them, I would wonder who could love them so much that they would encase them in glass for protection and to display their beauty. But once they were gone, I knew that security was an illusion.

I started school while living with Abuela. When I started first grade, I walked to school alone. My mornings would begin with me getting dressed, eating breakfast and then out the door. The day that I wore the yellow cotton dress that Abuela had made for me started as any other day. I began walking up the hill toward the school, but felt fearful and noticed no one seemed to be in the area. Maybe I was late, or maybe I was early, but no other school children were around and I knew that this was unusual. I walked with my books in hand as quickly as my little legs could take me. Then I noticed them—two teenage boys about two blocks behind me. What caught my attention was the large German shepherd they had with them. I was very fearful of big dogs, so I wanted to get away from them as quickly as I could. The faster I walked, the faster they walked. Then it seemed they were right behind me. Somehow, I could feel that something wasn't right, but where could I go? I was alone, surrounded by tall apartment buildings. Then I heard one of the boys yell at me, "Hey you! Stop!"

My heart began to run before my legs knew what to do. I heard someone running after me. My heart was screaming *boom-run, boom-run, boom-run* in my ears! I saw the dog from the corner of my eye. Then he was in front of me, growling. His presence stopped me and for a second I thought that my heart had stopped beating too. I stared at him and thought, *He is going to eat me if I move.* It felt as if I was standing for an eternity when the boys came running up behind me.

"Why were you running, little girl? We just want to talk to you." I'd never seen those boys before, nor would I ever see them again. They seemed cloaked in a dark cloud. "So where are you going?" they asked, not really caring for an answer. "Didn't you hear us calling you?" Again, no answer was necessary. The second boy poked at my arm. "Hey, do you talk?" They began laughing at my fear. I stared ahead, not knowing what was coming next. "Hey, you're cute," said the second one.

The first one owned the dog and told the dog to come to him. The boy saw that I was terrified of the dog and said, "If you don't move, he won't bite you." At that moment I was caught, paralyzed by fear. "Hey, do you want to play?" asked the second boy. "We know this great game that will make you feel good." The first boy laughed and agreed with him. "Come with us, and we will show you our game." I couldn't move, but they pushed me and laughed. I held my books tightly as they pushed me into an alley between two buildings. I could see the dark entrance getting closer, and somehow I knew that whatever was in that alley was coming for me.

Once they pushed me into the alley, they knocked my books

out of my hands and started to laugh. Their laughter was sinister and seemed baited by the darkness that surrounded us. They began telling me sexual secrets little girls should never know. They opened their pants to show me their privates, somehow knowing that I had never seen that before. They yanked my dress up and removed my white cotton underwear. Then they both began to do things that no little girl is ever ready to endure.

My mind had learned to leave during difficult times, so I left. I could hear their laughter. I could hear the things they were saying, but my body and mind weren't mine anymore. I had gone and I couldn't look at Little Girl Me. I don't remember how long it took or everything that happened. Once they were done, they demanded my lunch money. I looked down at my hand. There in the palm of my hand was a shiny nickel. The second boy followed my eyes and grabbed it while laughing. His inside joke was lost on me. They had done all this for a nickel. The destruction of my child's innocence was worth just a nickel. My mind wandered back to those dolls lying on the floor. I knew that there was nothing I could do to put them back together again. No amount of glue, no amount of hands, no amount of love would ever make them beautiful again.

I could feel His presence. My abuela talked about Him enough that I knew Him. It wasn't an angel, it was Him, coming to save me. But was He too late? Would He see my worth? Did He know that I was only worth a nickel? I could feel His hand as I walked to school without underwear. My dress may have covered my nakedness, but looking at me from afar I looked exposed. My eyes were gone. In their place was a deep darkness. Somehow I had swallowed the thing that had lingered in that alley. I grabbed His hand tighter, hoping to go with Him, but He wouldn't immediately let me leave. He walked with me to school. I got in trouble for arriving late, so they called my abuela but allowed me to remain the rest of the day. He didn't have to speak. His hands spoke volumes. He caressed my head when the school administrator yelled at me for being late. He sat next to me as my brain tried to listen to the teacher and forget the images

21

corrupting the innocence of my mind. He walked home with me as fear wrapped its fingers around my mind as I imagined the teenage boys coming back for me. He pacified my abuela's anger when she began asking questions: "Where were you? Where did you go?"

But how could I explain something so unexplainable. At dinner she watched me look at my plate as if I were waiting for someone else to come and eat for me. Frustrated, she sent me to my room with little to say except "Go." I usually loved her food, but I couldn't eat. A stone had been placed in my stomach, cold and heavy, leaving no room for food. I walked into my room, a shadow of what used to be me. I sat on my bed and noticed my bare bottom touching the sheets. "Please can I go now?"

I sat with Him in silence. Abuela looked in on me. Her eyes seemed worried, but I was too far gone to care. I squeezed His hand again, this time as hard as I could and He nodded His head as He looked at Abuela. For a moment, I believed that she too could see Him. I thought she would come over and ask Him, "What's wrong with her, Jesus? Can you help her?" But instead, she silently closed the door.

As He took me away, I looked at Little Girl Me and saw her lie down on the bed. She pulled her legs to her chest and began sucking her fingers. I could hear her humming a song my abuela had taught me. Tears filled my eyes as I watched her. I wanted to go to her and say something. But what did I know? I squeezed His fingers again as I turned away. I could hear Little Girl Me humming to Jesus a child's gospel song, slow and easy. "Yes, Jesus loves me. Yes, Jesus loves me. Yes, Jesus loves me. The Bible tells me so."

But I was six years old and I hadn't read the Bible. I was humming it, hoping that somehow He would reveal the truth of that song to me. By taking me away, I guess He did.

CHAPTER 5

Pinocchio Hopes

> Hope deferred makes the heart sick …
> —Proverbs 13:12

I lived with Abuela until the age of six or seven. There were good days and bad days after my incident. I never opened my mouth about it, but my head wouldn't shut up. Who would believe a story from such a childish little girl? So I locked it up, deep inside, right beside my dead mother. I knew no one would find it because no one ever pried deep enough into my heart to see what was going on. I was just a child with silly ideas and silly thoughts. Who would want to dig so deep as to find these dead bones? Then they would be responsible to raise them up again. Who would care enough to do such a thing?

Abuela was my first casualty. We became distant even when sitting in her narrow kitchen. When she sang to Christ, her Savior—I would mouth the words but dared not make a sound. Speaking and laughing also suffered and came less and less. Something had changed in Abuela too. She wouldn't let me go to school alone anymore. She started sending me with the neighbor's children, who were older than me. Then one day, my uncle Bobby showed up

23

with his slow swagger, smiling at me as if I were something to smile about. He started walking me to school, and in his presence, I dared anyone to come and mess with me. He showed me kindness and patience. I drank it in like the sun on winter ground. It felt good to have a man show me any kind of goodness and he did it freely. He would read to me and play games at a time when adults rarely took much interest in me. Abuela had to work long hours and she went to church just about every day. My aunt was involved with her boyfriend and friends, so Uncle Bobby and I were left alone a lot, and that was all right with me.

My uncle's hair was dark and shiny. His dark eyes seemed to glow. He talked and laughed with me about the silliest things. I would sit in Abuela's kitchen while he made us breakfast. My uncle always seemed present, unlike my abuela, who seemed programmed on the next thing. He hung out with me, often saying, "Little Rebekah, you are so beautiful. You are the most beautiful little girl I have ever seen." Oh, how my heart soared. I couldn't hear anything he said after that. I was stuck on being the most beautiful girl, words never spoken over me by any man before.

Somewhere in my heart I tried to take ownership of those words, but in the process of growing up, they slipped out. I tried to lock them deep in a place where no one could see or touch them, but locks made in childhood open easily by adult hurts. But for that moment, it felt good to be loved so he instantly became my favorite adult male. To my child's eyes, he was the most handsome man I had ever seen. While my aunt's boyfriend would also show me attention, I knew that he was her boyfriend. Not that I understood the concept of boyfriend, but I recognized that my aunt had some kind of claim on him. As for my uncle, to my knowledge no one had any claim on him, so I claimed him, and he became my father-uncle.

Every morning my abuela would go to her shop, leaving me alone with him, which was a treat for me. He would make me breakfast, which most times consisted of cereal, but it was his smile that I looked forward to every day. The cereal tasted better than it had the day before because of his smile. He was good and safe, and he thought I was beautiful.

One specific morning I remember more clearly than any other. He had made me a hard-boiled egg. I didn't like eggs, so when he gave it to me, I just glared at it. You would have thought he had given me poop. My face contorted. I couldn't even handle the aroma, so I sat there with a sour face, holding my nose.

He looked at me and laughed. "What's wrong? Don't you like hard-boiled eggs?"

"No," I said, "I don't like eggs at all."

He looked at me with both surprise and amusement. "Don't like eggs, huh? I don't know anyone who doesn't like eggs."

"Well, I don't," I said.

He didn't become impatient, he didn't try to make me eat it, and he didn't tell me about the children in Africa dying to have food—all things that my previous father would do or say to make me eat. No, my father-uncle Bobby sat next to me and added pepper to the already salted egg. Now, I had tried eggs with salt but never pepper. He said, "Try it with pepper. This really makes it taste better. I promise. If you don't like it, I'll give you cereal." He had given me a choice and he spoke with kindness. No one had ever given me a choice before.

I gladly tried the egg with pepper and found that he was telling the truth. Eggs with pepper did taste better. How did he know that? To my six-year-old mind, he had created a miracle. Others had tried to force, convince, cajole and even preach me into eating eggs, but none had succeeded. All my father-uncle did was give me a choice and add some magic black powder, and *bam!* I was now an egg-eater.

He smiled as he watched me eating. "You see? It's good, isn't it?" I looked across the table at him, where he had prepared his own eggs. "See? I knew you would like it because you're like me. I don't like eggs without pepper either." He said this as casually as breathing, but oh, it hit my heart like a first kiss. The thought that we were alike left me a little dizzy as I sat watching him eat. My heart jumped, and I knew that he was the one who would save me one day, with a pepper shaker in hand, sprinkling all things bad and making them good. Silly, I know, but I was only six, and heroes were hard to find.

Living near Yankee Stadium was a special treat. While my father-uncle stayed with us, he took me to my second game. Abuela's husband, John, had taken me to my first game. John was a very soft-spoken man, and his presence was almost nonexistent in Abuela's house. Although he was peaceful, and I believe that he was trying his best to be thoughtful, his invisible presence left me with little memory of him. I believe he worked and helped my abuela, but she was a force that swallowed his soft presence. He rarely spoke to me, so when he took me to the game at Yankee Stadium, I was happy and surprised.

But my best time was with my father-uncle. I don't know if father-uncle liked baseball, but he seemed to be enjoying it with me. He got me a hot dog and soda and I was in heaven. The day seemed brighter than usual. It was warm but not uncomfortable. Although we were surrounded by thousands of people, I felt like it was just him and me. I could hear him yelling at the umpire and cheering for his team, the Yankees.

I mimicked everything he did so he would send me approving smiles, making me feel warmer on the inside. My time with my father-uncle was good and pure. I was allowed to be a child, and he was allowed to be my uncle. He never asked anything of me, but he always gave without taking.

My aunt's boyfriend, Nick, was also kind but in a less present way. After my father-uncle had gone, I tried to replace him with Nick, but he didn't live with us, so our time together wasn't as distinct as my uncle's. Whenever he came over, his attention was divided between my aunt and me, but that was okay by me because I loved my aunt and wanted her to be happy too. They would take me out for ice cream or to the park. We lived near the park and would take long walks there, or I would play on the swings and jungle gym while they watched. At these times, I felt wanted. Despite my incident, I still maintained a child's spirit. I wanted to be loved and taken care of, and they seemed willing.

One day after we had been to the park, we came back home to my grandmother's cooking. My aunt joined my grandmother in the kitchen, leaving Nick and me alone, which was rare. In the living room, he read me a story from one of my favorite books, *Pinocchio*. I read this story so many times that I had it memorized, but I wanted to hear it through his voice. He read it with all the emotion of a fine actor. I laughed and became worried at just the right moments of the story. He was as into it as I was and that made that moment special. Once we finished the story, we were called in for dinner. I walked in with him and felt on top of the world. What a wonderful day it had become, and it was even better when he asked me, "What do you want me to bring you the next time I come?"

I knew instantly what I wanted. "A Pinocchio coloring book!" I answered.

He smiled and said, "Okay, you got it." I loved everything to do with Pinocchio. I had read the book over and over and would even dream about the story. Pinocchio's father's love was so deep for him that his father risked his own life to find Pinocchio. No matter what Pinocchio did, his father never gave up on him, never would let him go, and never let his hopes for his wooden boy diminish. Pinocchio, being a curious little boy, got into a lot of trouble, even giving away his schoolbooks, a gift his father had given him through great sacrifice. With the help of the fairy and the love of his father, Pinocchio was able to find his way back home.

Was I too young to understand all of this? I don't know. I loved the fact that Pinocchio was loved despite his wayward ways and that his father never gave up on him, not even when he ended up in the whale's belly. I wanted a coloring book with that story in pictures that I could color. I believe that Nick wanted to get it for me, but he never did. I waited for that gift until I left Abuela's home.

My real father had told her that he wanted me to come home.

By this time, he had moved away from Paterson, New Jersey, and had moved to Lancaster, Pennsylvania, where he had remarried. I couldn't wait to see my brothers, especially my little brother. I thought that I had been found, like Pinocchio. I thought that my dad had searched for me and had found me at Abuela's house.

Although Nick never got me the coloring book, and I never understood then, I understand now. He was in the air force. Life for an adult is bigger and more complicated than a child's need for a coloring book. But for me, a coloring book made the difference between feeling cared for and being forgotten. I often thought of my Pinocchio coloring book and my uncle. I never heard from my father-uncle again and wondered what had become of him. Long after our time together, while visiting my aunt, I found out. While living in Puerto Rico, my father-uncle was murdered; he was found hanging in a small wooden shack. By this time, my life hurts were so many that I didn't understand the magnitude of his death.

My Pinocchio hopes were long gone, replaced by the hard truth that no one was coming to save me. However, in a small way, he really isn't dead to me. Every time I eat eggs, which is still rare, I pick up the pepper shaker, and my heart goes to that small kitchen. In my mind's eye, I see him holding a pepper shaker, smiling, and saying, "I promise it will be good." Would he be telling me that right now, if he were watching me write this book? I don't know, but I wonder.

CHAPTER 6

Sweets and Dreams

When you lie down, you will not be afraid;
when you lie down, your sleep will be sweet.
—Proverbs 3:24

I believed that my father was coming for me. My abuela had said that he had gotten married and that he was soon coming to pick me up. I was excited to see my brothers but that excitement was always dampened by the realization that my father had killed my mother. My memory often replayed his outbursts and I still felt the imprint of his hands on my face. Lying in bed, I'd look up to speak to God. "Is my father different now? Has he changed, or is he still angry with me?" Somewhere in my mind I had reconciled that my father was mad at me. His words never felt kind and his face appeared scarred by a permanent scowl.

I had not slept well since my abuela mentioned he would be coming for me. On this night, somewhere between the light of day and the dark of night, where gray comes to take us away, I fell into a deep sleep. It felt as if I hadn't been asleep very long when I was stirred awake by a soft breeze. Bits of my hair tickled my face as I opened my eyes. I was lying in a field of tall grass and flowers. Turning my head slightly to the right I could see Him on a rock about seven feet away. His eyes were closed and the wind was lightly tossing His hair. I stared at him for a moment. He smiled without looking at me. He knew I was awake and staring at Him, but He was enjoying this moment, and so was I. I turned my face to the sky and looked at the purple tail of His glory dancing in the brightness of the sky. The light was so radiant that staring too long was impossible without feeling blinded. From a distance, sounds of music and song blew in with the breeze and danced with the scent of honeysuckle and bubble gum. I closed my eyes and sat in a presence that I knew was greater than anything I had experienced before. Without looking, I knew He was now staring at me so I smiled. I heard His laughter and the sound bounced off the walls of my heart with a love that embraced me completely. I looked at Him with my own laughter in tow.

Oh, how I enjoyed our time together. He rose from His large rock, walked toward me, and stopped at my side. He bent down and extended His hand. I rose, grabbed His hand and He pulled me to my feet. We were back in our secret place, but this time He surrounded me with flowers as far as my eyes could see. I heard the sound of our stream, so I looked beyond Him, and there it was. The water seemed to glisten with assorted jewels of many colors that flowed to a place I couldn't see. I looked back at Him and smiled. Around us were bits of gold sailing through the air, never landing but always floating. Whenever the brightness of the light would catch them, they would sparkle, reminding me of lightning bugs. The day felt neither hot nor cold; it just was. As we walked, a path formed. Worn down by others who had walked there before, it had become dusty, but we followed it, never speaking but hearing the song of life that surrounded us. He hummed the song and looked at me with a smile. I joined Him in this beautiful melody and closed my eyes, as I often did in Abuela's kitchen. The song was unfamiliar, but I knew it because He knew it.

He released my hand and touched my head. Security, love,

kindness, and goodness flooded my every cell, and flashes of me came to my mind's eye. Places and things never seen and never experienced flowed in and out of my being. Then we stopped, and I opened my eyes. There before me was a candy store. Large windows displayed what was inside. My heart felt restless. We entered without entering and I stood in the aisle. I slowly looked around me, taking in all that seemed perfect and good. Candy of all colors, flavors, and shapes surrounded me, encased in large glass jars that were full to the brim and seemed to glimmer. The walls were pink-and-white stripes while polished wood counters surrounded the store. The shelves of candy seemed to go up and up with no end, yet I could see them all. From the corner of my eye, I saw an angel appear. He was dressed in white with a white soda jerk hat. He seemed to be waiting for me. There were fountains ready to pour whatever I wanted. Somehow I knew that this was all for me but the gift overwhelmed me and left me stuck on the wooden floor. He, understanding my impasse, said, "So what would you like? Anything you desire, Rebekah, I'll give you. All you have to do is ask." He pointed to the angel behind the counter, who seemed ready to burst, and said, "He is here to serve you."

The joy on the angel's face as he looked at me reminded me of parents watching their child walk for the first time. But I couldn't walk. I couldn't move. My mind had found its way back to my shame. I could see the nickel in my hand. I knew that I didn't have enough for anything He had offered me. Here I was in His presence, looking at His promises, but all I could do was think about that darn nickel. He kneeled before me and looked straight into me. "Believe in me, Rebekah. I can give you something new." But I wouldn't look at him. All I could do was look at my hand that held that nickel.

I heard my name being called from somewhere far away. Although I hadn't moved, I looked again at my hand, and there was a large, pink, round ball. It was bubble gum. I loved bubble gum. "Go ahead; it's yours." As my hand moved to put it into my mouth, the call came again. "Rebekah, wake up!" I was gone before I could taste the sweetness of His gift, but I could smell its aroma. As I awoke, my hand clutched something that wasn't there anymore. When Abuela walked into the room, I was sad to be back in a place that wasn't my home. Why did He take me to beautiful places just to bring me back? I wanted to stay with Him and play with the other children that I had seen in my previous trips—children like me, broken, lost, unwanted, unworthy and worst of all, unloved by people who were supposed to care for them. There, I knew, was where I belonged and was loved. But I was back and the devil wasn't far away.

CHAPTER 7

My New World of Cows, Corn, and Crazy

The Lord will make you go crazy, make you blind,
make your mind confused.
—Deuteronomy 28:28

I waited for a couple of weeks, but my father never came for me. After a while, my abuela explained that my father was busy working and couldn't pick me up, so she decided to take me to him. That surprised me because no one seemed busier than Abuela, yet she was always available for me.

My abuela got us ready to go to Lancaster, Pennsylvania, to my father's new life. As we rode in her car and got closer to Lancaster, I feared she was taking me to another planet. Large buildings were replaced by rolling fields of corn and wheat. Mobs of people were replaced with what my abuela called cows. "That's where milk comes from," she would say. That grossed me out and generated curiosity about this new place. Then I saw them—people dressed like Pilgrims. They reminded me of the pictures my teacher had showed us when referencing the first Thanksgiving dinner. Why were these people dressed like this? Was Thanksgiving a daily ritual here? To say I felt out of place was an understatement. I looked at my abuela. She seemed as amused by them as I was confused. She smiled at the Pilgrims as she passed them. I hoped she wouldn't get too familiar with them. Our trip seemed to last forever, but eventually we stopped at a very small house.

"Well, Rebekah, we're here." But where was here? I couldn't see how my father and brothers could fit in such a small place. As we got out of the car, I looked around the neighborhood and noticed that all the houses looked the same. They were joined together, standing at attention like brick soldiers proud of their posts. Unlike the large buildings I was used to, these small homes seemed determined to show me their power of holding much within little space. They were warmer than my previous home and I fell in love with them before my feet touched the ground. My abuela, always two steps in front of me, was already halfway up the walkway toward the front door. I hurried, as I always did, and reached her side.

She gave me one final look. "Okay, Mama, here we are." She had never called me Mama before; that was my aunt's word for me. Her shoulders slumped a little and she put her hand on my head the way Jesus always did when we walked together. I felt her worry, which seemed strange because Grandma wasn't afraid of anything or anyone.

On one occasion when we were taking the elevator down, it stopped before our destination. Two masked men holding guns burst in yelling, "Give us your purses, wallets, and jewelry!" There were about five of us in the elevator. Panic pushed me behind Grandma, but she seemed to grow bolder and stared at the two men.

They noticed her staring and said, "Well, Grandma, give us your purse and ring." She simply looked at them, quickly opened her purse, took out her wallet and started to remove her driver's license.

"What are you doing, lady?" the other guy said, more shocked than angry.

"Getting my license. You don't need it, and I don't want to go through the trouble of getting a new one. So if you want the wallet, wait a second and let me get it out. " I stood behind her, shocked at her boldness. I was trembling and holding on to her, while she was having a conversation with two thieves with guns. I couldn't believe it. Everyone in the elevator turned to her with a look of disbelief and annoyance, but I felt fear for her. They tried to take her wedding ring, but once again she calmly explained, "This is my wedding ring. Please understand that my husband would not be too happy if I parted with it." I believe that the men were so shocked that they couldn't stop staring at her lack of fear. That was my grandmother.

On another occasion I saw her chase a man down after he reached into her car and took her purse. She put her car in park, and off she went, yelling, "Stop him! Stop him!"—and someone did. When she returned, she was still angry but satisfied that he had been caught.

So why would she show fear now? I could see tears forming in her eyes. My grandma seemed lost in this moment and the unfamiliar spirit brought me fear. "Be good, okay, Mama? Be nice to the new lady." I was struck by the thought that my abuela was thinking of her dead daughter. Did she think it was my fault she was dead? Was it because I wasn't good enough? I didn't have time to ask before the door opened. There stood this woman I had never met. She smiled at Abuela and asked, "El mana Ignacia?" (meaning "Sister Ignacia," my abuela's first name, I later found out). My abuela smiled back and said, "Sí" (yes). They did their usual hello as the woman opened the door and invited us in. She never looked at or acknowledged me. Abuela didn't seem to notice, but she introduced me. "This is Rebekah."

The woman then looked at me and introduced herself as Diana, my new mother. For a millisecond, pain flinched in Abuela's eyes, which created an insignificant twitch, too small for anyone but me to notice. Diana's eyes were small and dark and full of secrets, held back by a dam of shame. There was sadness in her spirit where her soul once resided but now was replaced by deep anguish and loss.

I looked at Grandma. Could she see it too? Abuela was engrossed in conversation, and Diana's Mary Jane taffy smile, which caught Abuela in its sticky sweetness, away from the truth in her eyes.

Looking away, I searched for my brothers. I found them at the top of the steps, looking down at us. They stood stiff and straight—or as straight as little boys could stand. My older brother, John, had an expression of happiness and apprehension mixed with anxiety. My little brother, Josiah, stood next to him but kept bouncing. When I looked at him, he smiled. He started down the stairs without being told, but John extended his arm in front of him and stopped him. Diana seemed to sense them; she turned, looked at them, and with her sweetest voice she called them. "*Vente* [Come]. Come down, boys. Your abuela is here." My brothers looked like little robots as they came down. I felt sorry for my little brother. He was so excited that he kept doing a mild form of the pee-pee dance. I assumed he was going to take off and the thought of that worried me. Diana eyed them the whole way down. As my little brother's dance started to escalate, I could see John's apprehensive eyes on her. "Go ahead hug your abuela."

They did as told, but I knew that they also wanted to hug me. Finally, Josiah couldn't contain himself anymore and broke rank to run toward me. He grabbed me and yelled, "My sisder!" He was four years old, and *sister*, I guess, was too difficult for his tongue to handle. Finally, John came from behind him and hugged me, but his eyes never left Diana's. I cried. I was happy to see them but sad at the familiar feelings that had entered into our reunion.

She then called another boy down. She introduced him to Abuela as James, her son. He was chunky and when he came to me, he shook my hand. His eyes had the same sadness as his mother, and I knew that my life was in for a change.

Abuela left with many tears from her and us. My heart sank at the sight of her car driving off. I saw her sit in her car for a few moments. I knew that she was talking to Him and asking Him to keep an eye out for us. But in this place, it felt almost hopeless to call on Him. The house felt dark and cold, even though it was summer and still daylight. Diana showed me to the room I was to share with Josiah. It was very small, with only a single set of bunk beds. She explained that I was to sleep on top since Josiah might tumble out and fall. Josiah was none too happy about that decision, but she made it final so it wasn't an option.

That evening when my father arrived, he said hello and smiled at me with tired eyes. He was a truck driver with long hours behind the wheel, which left him with little emotion to share. We were in the dining room that was small but held us well. Diana expected me to set the table, and her son seemed determined to help, which in a way was good because I had never done it before. Josiah wanted to help too, but Diana yelled at him to go upstairs. Her visceral irritation for Josiah was palpable in the way she spoke and looked at him.

We ate in silence. My father seemed disconnected from us and she was annoyed by his dismissive behavior. Breaking the silence, she would ask him questions about his job, but his short answers fueled her already seemingly senseless anger. After dinner, we were told to go upstairs. I was happy to go with Josiah to our room.

We sat on the bed and talked, laughed, and talked some more. John eventually came in and asked how I had been. He didn't act like an eight-year-old boy to me. He acted and spoke as if life had already given him too much, and the weight was crushing his child inside. Whenever he would speak, his words seemed covered with a film of sad disappointment. Although we were together again, spiritually, we were as dead as our parents' marriage; except for Josiah.

CHAPTER 8

Josiah the Darkness Slayer

Reaching into his bag and taking
out a stone, he slung it.
—1 Samuel 17:49

My little brother became my personal superhero. He didn't need a cape; he was wrapped in humor, mixed with laughter and adventure, and his powers made him unafraid of darkness. Others, like John and me, seemed helpless against the dark spirits in our home, but not Josiah. He seemed to stare them down and in the midst of despair, create joy. Where had my little brother gotten such powers? Looking at him reminded me of David, the giant slayer. But my brother's sling was formed of humor, and his stone was laughter that had the power to pierce into the darkest places and bring forth rays of light.

I was grateful for my brother's company in our room because he always made me laugh. The years I spent alone at Abuela's created a craving in me to be around other people. My brother was two years younger than I was, but his awareness was older than most boys his age. His greatest gift was his knack to create laughter where tears once resided. I, of course, was happy to be his best audience. Any new performance he tried would create great amounts of laughter and joy in me. But we constantly needed to be aware of Diana's presence. Even our laughter would create overt bouts of annoyance, so we found ourselves hiding from her wherever we could.

Our days were an endless game of avoidance of fire. Diana had conjured an image of how we were supposed to act but had forgotten to clue us in. So we (especially Josiah and I) were constantly in trouble. John's presence was quiet, so he barely disturbed her equilibrium. At eight years old, his child spirit had dried; little was left of his little boy. I would look at him and could feel the weight of sadness that had pressed down on him, creating a lesser version of himself. The pain was too much sometimes, and he would lose his balance. Rolls of rage and anger would push against his chest and explode, striking our new older stepbrother. John's demotion brought him great confusion. He was the older brother, but now he was in the middle and reduced to taking orders instead of giving them. I understood because I was stuck in the middle too and overlooked. But he had never been there before, so for him, it was an unbearable pain to swallow. I wanted to help him, but he was too far gone. Any help from me was met with rage and anger. He began to fight in an attempt to show his proper status, but James always won the battle, even when my brother had won the fight—Diana made sure of it. One word to our father would propel my dad into a fury, and he would beat John back into submission. Then the dead-quiet boy would return for a while, until the next bout of truth would hit him and bring him back to life, even if it meant beating on someone. My father never asked my brother for his truth. John was exceptional in school. He was able to skip a grade because of his brains, but his temper kept him locked inside a place of lack. But Josiah and I— especially Josiah—got the worst doses of their madness.

Although the ZIP code had changed, the demons of the past were able to find us. Diana's pernicious spirit seduced my father's wrath toward us. There were instances when she couldn't control the demon wolf in my father. She would become his full moon and trigger his lycanthropic disease, and insanity would break loose in our small house. He would beat her, us, the walls, the furniture—anything that was in his way would suffer the craze of his disease. The next day our home would welcome the morning sun with smashed chairs, busted walls, and broken and bruised children. Diana would replace the furniture, my father would eventually repair the holes but no one cared to restore our hearts. But Josiah didn't need restoration; he had superpowers, and it was during these times that they shined best.

At night he would put on a great show for me. He would imitate my father's anger and broken English as he walked around the room, knocking things down, and saying things like, "I going to bee jew" (meaning "I'm going to beat you"). He would pretend to chase me and hit me. Both of us were bruised on the outside, but on the inside we had produced joy. Josiah's gift gave me laughter, when in the natural we should have been feeling sorry for ourselves. After a while, we couldn't help ourselves; our laughter would bubble out between the cracks of our bedroom door and spill down the stairs, irritating first Diana and then my father.

Sometimes John would come in and try to shut us up. "Shhhh! Dad's going to come up and hit you guys. Stop!" But his attempt at playing big brother had lost its magic, so all we had left for him was laughter. We didn't mean to make him feel bad. We were just children, lost by the hopelessness of the situation and trying desperately to find something to fight with, so laughter became our weapon of choice. He would leave angry and dejected, and his dejection created more comedic froth for us. Our father would come upstairs with gurgles of impatience, bolstered by Diana. Taking off his belt, he would enter our room and begin to swing it as if he were killing ghosts from his past, seen only by him.

Josiah was a great actor, and he would yell at the top of his voice, "Papi [Daddy], no! Papi, no! Please don't hit us!" This would irritate my dad enough that he would stop and yell at Josiah, "Jew be quwiet." When my father was done and had gone downstairs, I would hear Josiah giggling. I knew, without looking, that his face was pressed against the pillow. My father had given Josiah's gift more ammunition. At the realization, tears mixed with giggles would roll down into my own pillow. Tomorrow night's performance, I knew, was going to be a good one. It would star my dad again, but it would include a special performance featuring Josiah, the darkness slayer.

CHAPTER 9

My Companions, Shame and Worthlessness

I live in disgrace all day long, and my
face is covered with shame.
—Psalm 44:15

There were times when Diana tried to show kindness, but it seemed difficult for her. She wasn't comfortable in her own skin and even less so at being our mother. I wondered if her own fatherlessness and her first husband's abandonment might have created such brokenness in her heart that the chasm was too big for anyone to fill. Sometimes she would say kind words or treat us to something special to eat. But when my father was home, she would look at him like a child longing for approval. Maybe she had hoped that her kindness toward us would turn his attention toward her, but it never worked. My father wasn't demonstrative toward her, and his passion was limited. Her desire for more love from him and his lack of fulfilling her desire seemed to only fuel her anger toward us. He never gave her what she needed, so she never gave him what he wanted—a woman who would love his children. Being limited by my age, I didn't understand. All I saw was a woman who was possessed by passion that had no place to go, so it became twisted and its energy created resentment that poisoned her core. There were times when I would hear Diana calling out to God like my Abuela used to do, but her words were devoid of power and sounded more like possession. I could hear her repeating my father's name, so I often wondered what god she was calling. She wore her hurt plainly on her face, so sometimes I would feel sorry for her. I felt especially sad for her when my father would come home and overlook her hungry eyes to feed his own belly.

One of those days, when she was possessed by her need for him, he came home hungry, tired and disconnected. No matter what she said, he wouldn't give her what she needed, so my brother became her token sacrifice. Diana would hide food from us and keep it for herself and her son. Josiah had found her stash and because he was hungry, decided to eat a little. Diana went on a rampage and made up a story of what Josiah had done. She exaggerated her grievance so that by the time she was done, my little brother was close to being a murderer. My father asked her to be quiet, but this only escalated her anger. Josiah, John, and I trembled in our room; waiting for what we knew was coming.

My father called Josiah downstairs. My father stood by the steps while Diana was raging behind him. Before Josiah touched the last step, my father grabbed him by the shirt, picked him up, and threw him across the room. Josiah looked like a rag doll as he hit the wall. I was already halfway down the stairs when I saw my father kick my brother, who was lying limp on the floor. He kicked him so hard that I heard all the air come out of Josiah. Without any thought, my mouth opened and I screamed, *"Stop it! You're going to kill my brother!"* My legs moved without my brain's permission, and within seconds I was holding my father's legs. Josiah was desperately trying to breathe. John sat lost on the steps, crying and screaming at my dad. But my father's storm wasn't done. He grabbed me by the hair and threw me across the room. I could hear John begging my dad to stop.

My dad then turned to Diana and asked her, "What do you want me to do? Kill them?" When I heard him say that I knew that he would do it if she asked. Her silence enraged him, so he turned and walked outside. She followed him and begged him not to leave. He grabbed her by the hair and dragged her down the sidewalk. By the time she came back, she had holes in her clothes—and in her mind. My brothers and I had gathered in our small room. Diana walked into our room; she looked worse than we did. She walked up to me, pointed her thin bloody fingers at me, and said, "This is all your fault. You are evil, and you need to leave." She wasn't yelling. She barely opened her mouth, but she bared her teeth when she said it, like a wild animal wanting to eat its prey but unable.

Looking at her, I felt immense fear. I could hear my heart beating in my ears. In that moment, her hatred for us was so intense that not even Josiah would make fun of her. Her presence was devoid of light. The black in her eyes had taken over every part of who she was and created in her a cavern of bile. I could feel it oozing on my flesh like roaches. It crawled all over me, but no matter how hard it tried, it couldn't get inside, so it bore little holes of hatred on my skin. When she left, I could see that some had splashed on my brothers. They sat on the bed shivering, rubbing their arms as if removing imaginary insects. They both turned to me, and for the first time I saw hopelessness in Josiah's eyes. Maybe it was then that we finally realized that our father could kill us. I wondered if they knew about our mother but never dared to ask.

The next day Diana persuaded my dad to remove me from their home. Within a couple of weeks, I was gone. No reason was given, just "Pack your bags. You're going to your aunt's house." My aunt was my father's sister, someone I had never met. Good-bye was a heavy word to say and would get stuck between the back of my throat and tongue. The day I left, no one saw me out. My father took me in his truck early in the morning, before the sun rose. Josiah peeked out from under the blanket but didn't dare say a word. As I walked out, I could see Diana standing in the dining room, watching. I climbed in my father's truck, and we drove for what seemed an eternity. He dropped me off as if he were dropping off a load of cargo. "Well, here she is, and thanks for taking her." He walked away and never looked back at me, nor did he say good-bye. My aunt had just married and they lived in a small apartment. I barely was in the front door before I was quickly introduced to a life crazier than the one I'd left.

Their verbal fights quickly turned violent and physical. My aunt's husband would beat her, and she would beat him. Dinner would turn into plates flying, hot water being thrown, and knives taking dangerous flight. In the middle of this, I decided to mentally leave. Jesus would come for me, but He had stopped taking me with Him, so I decided to go to darker places on my own. I lived with my aunt for less than a year, but for me it felt like an eternity. While there, I learned how to live within myself. I didn't have anyone—no brothers, no friends—feelings became a commodity I couldn't afford. I slept on a small cot near the kitchen. The kitchen was a bright yellow, but no matter how hard it tried the darkness overshadowed its color, creating an ugly ambiance muted in gray. Shame would come and sit on the cot with me paralyzing me. When my aunt and her husband were fighting, I tried to imagine myself somewhere else. Heaven didn't seem right for me anymore. I was deemed unworthy by something inside, and the abyss seemed more attainable. But even there, I would only sit at the edge. I could feel the heat, but I was caught in the in-between. Sometimes I could hear the sound of a familiar gurgle from below. It sounded like laughter, and I knew satan was laughing at me. But I didn't care. I felt nothing, so when he laughed, I laughed back, mocking him because I was empty inside, and he was too dumb to see it.

CHAPTER 10

Immanuel, My Uncle

The Lord is close to the brokenhearted and saves
those who are crushed in spirit.
—Psalm 34:18

My father's brother came for me during my time at my aunt's house. One day he showed up, helped me pack, and out the door I went. No good-byes. Their home resided in Hades, so my uncle came to bring me back to earth. Unfortunately, I didn't have enough emotion for my aunt. They wanted more than a little girl who felt nothing when they felt so much.

I had never met my uncle, but he seemed kind. When he smiled, it produced a thump in the place where my heart used to reside. He took me to a small apartment on a sunny street, somewhere near my father. Somehow I knew that God had sent him, so when he told me that his real name was Immanuel, I wasn't surprised. His nickname was Manny, which was what everyone called him, and he too had just gotten married. Walking into his home was like walking into Abuela's house. There were remnants of God's presence everywhere. As we entered, Manny's new wife smiled and welcomed us by the front door. She kissed her husband, which I'd never seen done before, and bent down before me and hugged me. I grew stiff, but she held on until my body accepted what my heart couldn't. His wife, Ruth, had green eyes and a soft face. When they looked at each other, love was mutually given and taken. Their flow was a dance between two people, invisible to everyone other than themselves. In its presence I felt good; I understood that this was what marriage was supposed to look like.

In the beginning after my arrival, I continued to mentally leave. At times I would catch a glimpse of Ruth's face, looking at me. She was sad whenever she looked at me, and I wondered why. People often came and went from their small apartment, and the flow seemed natural in this new place. They were very involved with their church ministry. Their kindness was given freely to anyone who walked into their home. Waking from my trance at times, it wasn't unusual for me to see new people. These people were kind and full of joy. I would sit and stare at their faces and wonder what made them look so happy all the time. I knew that money was an issue for Manny and Ruth, but it never consumed them.

A few months after my arrival, New Year's came and awakened me. It was 1970. The New Year was brought in by a small gathering in their home. People were in their living room, laughing and singing. Joy flowed so easily that it woke me from my zombie-like I watched from my small room as people sang and lifted their hands. Some would cry while others laughed, but the feeling in the room was united by one spirit—joy. I walked around in the small apartment, looking for my aunt and uncle. I found them in the kitchen, serving food. When I entered, they seemed surprised. The sadness that was in their eyes for me was replaced by joy. Looking at me, they smiled and asked if I wanted something to eat. For the first time in a long while, I noticed that I was hungry, so I ate.

After my awakening, I could feel the love they had for me and for each other but especially the love they had for God. I enjoyed reading and the sound of other children but found it difficult to connect. I found myself making up stories of their wonderful lives and interjected myself in them. Then I dared to believe that my aunt and uncle would be my saviors. I tried to be as good as I possibly could, but that wasn't always successful. On occasion I would get my dress dirty, and my uncle would spank me, but his wife would tell him not to spank so hard because I was just a little girl. Manny would come to me and apologize. I couldn't believe that an adult would say sorry to me. He would explain that my father had sent him money for my clothes, and he felt responsible to keep them nice. I understood his explanation, but it made me wonder if they wanted me. My stay with them was uneventful, and they seemed happy to have me there with them—that was, until the day that a missionary family came to stay with us.

It wasn't unusual for my aunt and uncle to have people in their home. I enjoyed hearing stories of miracles, lives changed, and the challenges our visitors faced in their mission field. It was always filled with wonder and I would listen with great curiosity. So I wasn't surprised to come home from school and find a new family in our home. This couple had a son who was sixteen years of age. He was always kind to me and I enjoyed having someone to play with. He paid a lot of attention to me and seemed to like talking to me. After a few days of hanging out with him, I felt totally at ease with him. My desire to be accepted overruled my senses, so when he started playing house I went along with him. One day when I arrived home from school, he was alone, but I didn't see anything wrong with it. Everyone trusted him, including me, and so when I saw him waiting for me, I felt special. He told me that the adults had gone to church and that they would be back in a couple of hours. I smiled at him. In my mind I was happy to be alone with him.

He asked me if I wanted to play house again. I enthusiastically said yes. I saw "the look" for a brief moment but didn't pay much attention to it because he was my friend. He smiled at me and asked me to come with him into the living room. There, we began to play as usual. He told me that he was hungry. I made him pretend food and we pretended to eat. I made him his pretend coffee. He said things like, "You are a very beautiful, wife," and I repeated his words, except I said "husband." (He had taught me these responses.)

Then something changed; he added to our game and said that we were going to bed. "Undress," he said, "because that's how wives and husbands sleep." So I did. He gave me a look, and it transported me back to a dark alley in New York City. I couldn't stop it. He began to touch me, and I laughed. I laughed and laughed and laughed. I laughed at the thought that the demons had found me. The demons were back and had gotten into my new friend. As I left Little Girl Me, I was in the midst of laughing. But her laughter had no joy. It wasn't like Ruth's laughter. She would laugh at my silly antics. Her laughter sounded sweet, like the rolling of cotton candy around the barrel. It would come in waves. I loved the sound of it, so I often tried my best to hear her laugh.

But my laughter had no light and was filled with despair. I cried and laughed, but he seemed too far gone in his lust to care. Why did these demons keep finding me? I wondered what Ruth and Manny would say if they walked in. The thought made me laugh even more. Then they would know who I really was. Then they would know my value. I left again and never came back until the day I was taken away. I heard them talking about me to someone on the phone. Later, I found out that it was my father. They told him how sad they were for me, how I never seemed to have a chance. The words "She never had a chance" made me sad. My father came a week after their phone conversation. They had explained to me that they were about to have a baby and couldn't take care of me too. The sight of my father brought me new anxiety. He acted happy to see me, but I could also see the apprehension in his stare.

I was taken back to the home I had first seen with my abuela years ago, but this time its darkness was met by a deeper sorrow. I entered, aware that something was different, but I didn't know what it was. In my mind's eye I saw a sign on the door that read "Enter at your own risk," but I had nowhere else to go, so I entered.

CHAPTER 11

Dr. Jekyll or Mr. Hyde

Such a person is double minded
and unstable in all they do.

—James 1:8

When I returned, I saw that nothing had changed, yet everything had changed. The house was the same, but the people within had lost something that resembled their minds.

I was back in my old room but without my brother, who, they reasoned, was too old to be sharing a room with his older sister. I was welcomed back by a single dresser and a twin bed, flanked by shame and worthlessness. I stayed in my room until I heard my brothers arrive. I saw Josiah and John and was struck by the way their shoulders hung, as if they had worked all day in a rock quarry. Josiah looked particularly older, but something deeper had changed. As the day went on I could see that the power my little brother once had had turned in on itself. He seemingly was still funny, and anyone looking in would say so. But I saw the change and I wondered what had happened. His humor now had a touch of bitterness. If Diana told him he couldn't do something, he would do it quicker; if my dad told him to stop hitting, he would hit harder.

But what was most disconcerting was the way he would bang his head against the wall.

My older brother thought he was funny. James would egg him on. The adults thought he was acting stupid. They all laughed at him, and the louder they laughed, the harder he would bang. He was doing it so often that I noticed a lump the size of a gumball permanently fixed in the middle of his forehead. After banging his head, Josiah would turn and laugh with everyone while a bruise formed in the center of his forehead. He pretended that it didn't hurt, but the look in his eyes spoke of a deep pain he couldn't verbalize. Sometimes he would start again—*bang, bang, bang*—and then he would turn, seeking approval. Small amounts of blood would drip slowly down his cheeks, following the outline where tears once flowed. The weapon that once brought us so much relief, he used now to bring himself physical pain. What had happened to my little brother?

My father was home less and less, and when he was there, he would sit with glazed eyes, watching television. During baseball season, he would play until late into the evening and then go play dominos. Diana deteriorated in my father's absence, and her loneliness drove her to pace in our small living room. The creaking of the wooden floors as she went back and forth, back and forth, back and forth, could be heard upstairs and would lull me to sleep. I sensed that the same demons that kept my father away were keeping her mind running after him. I could feel her anxiety, and sometimes she would pray her hopeless prayers to a god that had no power.

At these moments I felt a deep sadness for her desperation, but I also felt resentment toward her. She wanted my dad to be her god, but he was a broken man whose only power was her weakness for him. My father scarcely had been around for a couple of days when Diana's heart finally had enough. It was three o'clock in the morning when she came into our rooms and woke us up. She dragged us outside in our pajamas and told us to walk the four blocks to the club and bring our dad back. John knew the way from past experience, so we followed him.

We entered a smoke-filled room full of people, laughing, drinking, as well as playing cards and dominos. The room went silent when we entered. I guess the sight of children in pajamas was an unusual one. My father looked up from a game of dominos. His face turned a dark red. John tried to explain, but my father yelled and told us to go back home. We feared him more than Diana, so we did what he said and walked back the four blocks. We knocked on the door, hoping she would allow us in so we could crawl back into our beds.

Diana peeked through the door and said, "Where is your father?" Her nose flared and her eyes were wild. Maybe it was because it was dark outside, or maybe it was because I was tired, but at that moment I hoped that she would let us in.

"He said that he wasn't coming back and that we should go back home," John explained as calmly as he could.

She became irritated. "Then you are all going to stay out there until he comes home!"

We looked at each other for a few moments. We didn't understand, and we were too tired to care. Without a tear or a word, we lay down on the concrete porch and fell asleep. We huddled together, three little lumps pressed together against a dark cool night that promised nothing new. Lying against each other, I could hear my brothers' heartbeats; their rhythm seemed like my own. It played a sad beat, hoping for a better day but knowing that today wouldn't be that day.

Our father's yelling and cursing awakened us. He banged on the door and cursed at Diana. He didn't use his key; he kicked the door down. Diana never remembered that doors couldn't stop my father's rage. Inside, he chased after Diana, who had waited for him all night on the sofa. We could see the light of dawn, and its fire seemed to ignite my father's rage. As he ran after Diana, we ran inside and hid. The sofa, table, and chairs became our safe haven. Diana decided to go into their bedroom and lock the door. I could hear my father breaking it down. He began beating her while she screamed his name, begging him to stop.

We tried our best to stay quiet, hoping he wouldn't notice us this time. He dragged her down the steps, cursing her while she begged him to stop. The rhythm of my heart had picked up a sound of warning. I could see my brothers in their hiding spot. I closed my eyes and tried to pray, but my father's and Diana's loud voices overpowered my own. I couldn't concentrate. Opening my eyes, I saw my father grab hold of my brothers. He began beating them as they screamed. He turned and his eyes met mine. His eyes were red. When he looked at me, I felt the warmth of my urine running down my legs. I knew he was coming for me and my fear kept me stuck to the floor. He knocked furniture over and grabbed me. We had betrayed him by obeying her. Once he was done, we ran into my room and once again huddled together, silently crying.

These moments of great fear and sorrow were forgotten when my father's anger was replaced with moments of genuine warmth and laughter. He would wrestle with my brothers and laugh with them. The sight of my father's smile was so rare that we would do anything to prolong it. I would stand on the sidelines and cheer them on. He was funny, and when he would hug me, the strength in his arms made me feel secure. My father enjoyed showing my brothers his strength. He always pinned them down, and no matter how hard they tried to pin him, he always won. I loved seeing my brothers laugh with my father while they rolled around on the floor. In these rare moments, my father would act silly and pretend to be a lion or an ape. Those were the moments I would go back to when everything looked bruised and broken. There, I could love my father and hope that he would return to that happy place. While I listened to him destroy our house, I would close my eyes and wish for our better day hoping maybe tomorrow it would come.

CHAPTER 12

They Call It Puppy Love

Let him kiss me with the kisses of his mouth-
for your love is more delightful than wine.
—Song of Songs 1:2

It was a Sunday, and my uncle had preached a sermon on salvation and damnation that was so good that I knew even the demons were trembling and considering repentance. My uncle said, "Everyone bow your heads. Does anyone want to receive the Lord tonight?" I bowed my head and considered repenting again. I repented at least once a month and couldn't remember if I had done my time this month. However, my curiosity took over, and I looked up. Families led by fathers gathered together, crying. I looked at the place where my father should had been, and my heart sank. It was baseball season, and my father had gone to his own church.

Every summer at the beginning of baseball season, my father would revert to trading his armor of truth for a baseball uniform. These seasons brought bouts of great pain and fighting in our home. Watching these families made my heart hurt. I longed for my father's presence, but it was baseball season, and his service started at the same time as ours. As I sat contemplating my father's choices, I felt a strange sensation, as if someone was watching me. I turned in time to catch a glimpse of a boy trailing behind his family as they walked down the aisle. His father was leading the family to salvation, but the boy lagged behind his two brothers and mother as he stared at me. His eyes were the color of muddy water and seemed too big for his face. His mouth was full of teeth larger than the space allotted for them, so when he smiled, his teeth seemed happy to be out. His smile had a power I'd never encountered.

I felt the bile coming up my throat, and my heartbeat was so loud that I couldn't hear anything but the sound of its pounding. I didn't smile back because I could barely breathe. I thought I was going to faint. I tried to tell Josiah, but my mouth was incapacitated. As he passed, my heart began to slow down, and my mouth remembered to function, but I had decided it was best not to mention it to anyone.

We went to church at least three times a week, and this new family started showing up. The new boy seemed to always find me. He would smile and wave at me, and all I wanted to do was punch him. Every time he waved, the motion of his hand created a hypnotic trance that affected the middle of my chest. My heart would find its way up my throat and I wanted to throw up. Hoping to discourage him, I began my own campaign. Whenever he looked at me, I would turn away and pretend not to see him. This would only make him smile, which irritated me even more. So I started sticking my tongue out at him. I thought, *That will show him.* But my heart wouldn't stop doing a crazy flip-flop motion.

I began to notice that I was watching for him. If his family didn't show, I felt sad. My new feelings over a strange boy made me angry with myself. I loved my brothers and even my father, but I had little to give. How could this boy be so selfish? By the third Sunday, the waving stopped. He no longer looked at me, so I kept my feelings to myself, but I felt a little heartache. Josiah had noticed my campaign had stopped. Without a word, he decided to speak to the boy's younger brother.

"What's your name?" Josiah asked.

The little boy smiled and said, "I'm John."

"How about your brother?" Josiah asked.

"Which one?" John said, looking at his brothers.

"That one." My brother's short finger pointed at the boy who had tormented me since the day they first walked down the aisle. I wanted to run away, but once again curiosity kept me watching.

John told him, "That's Nathan."

At the mention of his name, Nathan turned. Josiah waved and said hello and then walked back to me. "His name is Nathan."

I looked at my brother as if he had just told me some silly joke. "Why are you telling me?" I asked, staring him down as best I could. He looked back at me with a smirk, shrugged his shoulders, and walked away. I felt silly, but I was in it too deep, so I yelled, "I don't care. He's ugly."

At this, Nathan looked at me and smiled. He hadn't looked at me all night but before he entered his family's car, he looked and smiled. I wanted to take back my words, but they were out, and I had no way of taking them back

Josiah started to play with Nathan's brother John after church. They would run around, playing tag in the church parking lot. Other children soon joined them, including Nathan. I usually joined my little brother, but this time I couldn't. I stood back and watched. On Tuesday they played, and I watched. On Thursday they played, and I watched. By Sunday it seemed that all the children were playing together, but I was stuck watching.

I was standing against the church wall when Nathan came over. My legs felt like they'd been filled with sand and I couldn't move. "So why don't you play with us?" he asked.

I looked at him, trying my best to stare him down. "Because." It was all my head could think to say.

He looked at me like I had just stepped on his toes, "Because? Are you afraid?"

How dare he challenge me? I thought. I could feel my little fist form and I found strength returning to my legs. "Okay, I can play, but don't cry if I'm better than you."

He smiled and ran off. But before running off, he said, "Okay. Tag! You're it!" I was so mad I wanted to punch him. I ran after him until my father called for us to get in the car. My little brother thought it was brilliant the way Nathan had tricked me. I punched my brother in the arm and he laughed harder. I looked at him and couldn't help myself. His laughter was always contagious. I began to laugh too.

That week I joined in the games. Nathan and I seemed to be in a relentless game of our own. Some of the other kids complained, but we were having too much fun. He would tag me, and then I would tag him back. What once was boring became the best part of the week. I didn't understand the feelings I had for him, but I knew I wanted to be near him all the time. I would sing of the love of Jesus, and thoughts of Nathan would come to me. How could anything be better than what I felt for my new friend? With my new friend, I started to feel happy. I'd never felt so much before. His smile produced a deep hope in me. I didn't understand the bubbling of emotions going through me, but I knew it felt good.

Nathan looked at me as if I was worthy. He helped me forget the lies that had produced so much pain, so staying in this natural world became bearable. I danced alone in my room. Music wasn't necessary because the melody of hope made my body move. Nathan had seen me and thought I was worth his attention. Josiah would make fun of me, and I would tell him to stop being stupid. (My father called us *el stupido* all the time.) Deep inside, I enjoyed his poking fun of me because it involved Nathan. In every book I'd read, I'd change the male name to Nathan. He was always the hero, the savior, and someday he would save me. I formed a special world where he and I lived, and no one could hurt us. After two months of playing tag, we changed things and began playing hide-and-seek. Nathan was "it," so we all hid, but he always found me first.

Once, I was hiding in the alley between the buildings. While waiting in the darkness, I started to feel fear, so when Nathan found me, I tried to leave.

"Where are you going?" he asked.

"I don't like it here. It's too dark." I said it before I realized how silly I sounded.

"Don't worry. I'm here. No one can hurt you."

While standing under the floodlights next to the alley, I looked into Nathan's eyes. They had changed color since the first time I saw him. They were the color of honey, and I felt drawn to him. Within seconds of his promising his protection over me, he kissed me lightly and walked away. I just looked at him. A new sweetness had come over me, like extra hot fudge on a super duper sundae. My soul wanted to leave and walk away on its own. My heart, which contained a dam full of hurts, burst with happiness. Tears rolled down from somewhere deep inside, and touching the very lining of my being. In that moment, I was transformed from worthless to worthy. The world suddenly had color and sound.

Now I understood the song in my heart. The songs of the love of Christ now made sense. I knew that this was love. This overwhelming flow of emotions mixed with mountains of hope I wanted to climb began to swell within me. Everything seemed possible from this mountaintop. I felt high as I walked back to my father's car. Nathan had kissed me. This was my secret, and I put it deep in my heart and locked it deeper than any other secret I had. I wanted it to take root in me, to be looked at from this perspective and not from an unwanted girl's point of view. I knew Nathan liked me, and maybe this new realization would produce a truth that would open my father's heart. Maybe he would see me worthy. Maybe Diana would see that I was just a little girl, willing to do anything for love.

Sitting in the car, I smiled the whole way home. When we got home I went to my room and sat up half the night, looking out the window and telling Jesus, "Thank you for my new friend." It was the first time anyone had noticed me for me. Nathan never asked for anything nor did he ever take anything from me. He never tried to kiss me again. We played every day after church. He would run away and let me catch him, and we would stand around and talk. Silly words were exchanged, but I felt heard and wanted.

Two months later, my father decided to run off with another woman, and he left us behind with Diana. It was time for me leave again.

Diana and my dad would eventually get back together, and my brothers would return with them. I was not to return until several years later, and even then it was only for months at a time. Nathan's family continued to go to my uncle's church. Every time I was back in town, we would reconnect. When we were eighteen and ready to graduate from high school, Nathan asked my dad for my hand in marriage. It never came to fruition. After graduation, Nathan went into the marines, and life for both of us changed.

Breaking up was very difficult for me. My life spiraled out of control. Through my younger years, I loved Nathan because he showed me kindness at a time when I lived in deep darkness. My life went into aimless places after we broke up. A piece of who I thought I was supposed to be, died. But God restored in me a greater purpose, and now I see His wisdom in allowing our break up to happen.

CHAPTER 13

Big Boys Don't Cry But Sometimes Neither Do Girls

For I eat ashes as my food and
mingle my drink with tears.
—Psalm 102:9

B eing the only girl in a house full of boys should have had its advantages, but living senseless means that no one gets noticed, and everyone gets the pointless measure of obscurity. In this world, my brothers treated me like I was one of them because to them, I was. My gender made no difference to them because it made no difference to my father. The only one who noticed the difference was James, and he looked at me like his personal anatomy doll.

My brothers roughhoused with me and at times I enjoyed keeping up with them. John was very strong, and like my father, he had a way of letting us feel it. When we were playing with him, he would get so intense that we often would get bruised. I felt sorry for John. I often would see him alone, looking off into space, but I had become afraid of him. He would lose his temper while we were playing and end up punching us. His fist cradled the anger and frustration of all that he couldn't express, so when he landed his punches, it left an imprint of all he couldn't say. Our way of dealing with our own sense of guilt at mocking our brother, was to turn it into a game. Josiah had a talent of making the uncomfortable feel comfortable. Our fear of John, however, grew to the point that Josiah and I eventually stayed away from him. John stopped trying to hang out with us, and we stopped feeling guilty.

As his isolation grew, he became more and more introverted, and we became more and more numbed to his hurt. That's how we all survived. We killed off each other emotionally so that we could handle our own pain and not have to carry any more than we needed.

James was groomed to be a loner. He never played with my dad or with us. Diana kept him away from us, telling him that we were evil and that she didn't want him near us. James was a good boy and listened to his mother but he stopped listening when he started watching me. He began showing up in unusual and personal places when no one else was around. When I was in the bathroom, in the midst of doing my personal business, he would pop out from behind the shower curtain. He would wait until I had pulled down my underwear and was sitting on the toilet and then come out, laughing and watching me. I frantically tried to pull up my underwear while yelling at him, but he wouldn't move. I never had time to clean myself, so I left feeling ashamed at what he had done and unclean for what I couldn't finish.

At other times he would break into the bathroom while I was in it. He did this so often that I began to sneak into the bathroom in the middle of the night and get my personal business done then. My fear grew and it enabled me to hold what I needed to get done in the bathroom until night. After a while, I stopped taking showers and going to the bathroom during the day. There were times when I would urinate on myself. I would hide my underwear and wash them by hand, hoping no one would notice. He was relentless in his pursuit of me. I felt like an animal being hunted, but I was stuck inside his terrain. I knew that I didn't have a chance, and he seemed to enjoy the torment. Then one day, without notice, his behavior escalated.

That day, we weren't alone; he had a friend over, and I thought for a moment that I was safe. He had never done anything in front of anyone, but on this day, James and his friend pinned me down and began taking turns touching me. I tried to fight them off, but they were bigger. They tickled me to loosen my defenses. There were times when he would bring two boys to pin me down. Holding my legs and arms down allowed them to stick their hands into my private areas. They would all get their share, and after fighting and fighting, I would give up and start to laugh. My laughter came from a place of deep anguish. Once again, I left and watched Little Girl Me struggling.

God never came for me during this time; I didn't want Him to. My shame had become bigger than my desire for Him. In this place, I was neither happy nor sad. Emotions weren't a part of the environment. As a matter of fact, the fewer emotions I felt, the easier it was for me to stay away, and I stayed away for long periods. There, I didn't have to be anything to anyone. There, no one expected me to be good. I could see my surroundings, but it didn't affect me, so I laughed at those who tried to hurt me because I was gone.

James started getting bolder, entering my room in the middle of the night. I would pretend to be asleep, but nothing would stop him. One day his uncle came to visit us in our small house. All day I could see his uncle's eyes on me, and I knew what he was thinking. I dreaded going to sleep that night and prayed that night wouldn't come. But night always follows day, and after it swallowed the light, I knew that this night would be the worst.

I was asleep when they came. James had brought his uncle, and I heard them whisper. "Go ahead. No one will find out," James told his uncle as they crept into my dark room. I tried to be as still as possible, but that never mattered to James, nor did it matter to his uncle. He rolled on top of me while James cheered him on. "Come on; get up there. Hurry up." They laughed as if I were nothing more than a game they were trying to win. When his uncle climbed on top of me, I could smell the alcohol mixed with stale cigarettes. A nervous giggle leaked out of his mouth, and James told him to be quiet. His uncle seemed happy at their bonding experience. I left as he started speaking into my ear. He said things in Spanish that I couldn't comprehend, but I understood. I left Little Girl Me. I saw him on top of her and saw the words sliming all of his foulness on her, but I couldn't stay. Off I went to my space where nothing mattered.

Although I never called on God anymore, I could see Him out of the corner of my eye, but I felt angry and worthless and He wasn't welcome in that place. I looked at Him sideways, but our game had long since been replaced by a dark space.

That night I fell into a deep sleep until my father's voice woke me. He whispered in my ear, "Rebekah, it's okay." He picked me up and took me to his room, locking the door behind him. I heard his footsteps go down the stairs. They sounded angrier than usual. Loud arguing came rumbling up the stairs. I heard my father's rage and James's uncle's whimpers. I heard the familiar sound of furniture being thrown and Diana screaming, "Jim, no! Don't hurt him!" I heard James's uncle yelling and cursing at my dad. Then I heard what sounded like someone getting beaten. I could feel the familiar spirits rising and falling with each punch and kick. A little fear came rising from the pit of my stomach, but then I remembered what James's uncle had done. A strange calm washed over me like cool air blowing on hot embers. I realized that my father had found out what James's uncle had done to me and was beating him for it. I lay back, closed my eyes, and saw in my mind's eye all that was happening downstairs.

As I went under the covers, I smiled. It was the first time my father fought for me. It made me feel loved. That night I slept so soundly that when I woke up, I was back in my room and wondered if I had imagined it all. It wasn't until I went downstairs for breakfast that I knew I wasn't dreaming. The dining room had gotten quite a beating, and when Diana walked in from the kitchen, I saw that she had too.

Diana's dislike of me intensified after that and whatever kindness she had shown me in the past was now replaced with anger. She began finding reasons to complain to my father about me. He began beating my brothers and me, sometimes without our knowing what we had done. My father's beatings were so savage that I would urinate on myself before he even started. My legs would shake so violently that I would always end up on the floor. Once he was done, we were left black and blue from head to toe. Often I would go to school and church with a black eye, but he would always tell us not to tell. He would say that what happened at home was supposed to stay at home and that telling other people was a way of disrespecting him as a father. We never told, not even when people would ask about our black eyes. After a while, people would look at us like we were dumb and clumsy kids, and I guess that was okay with our father because he never said anything different.

After living with my father for almost a year, I thought this was where I was to live the rest of my life. Although our situation wasn't the best, I thought this was how most people lived. I never heard from Abuela or my aunt. I often wondered about them. I tried not to think too much about them because it made my heart hurt. It was enough that my body was hurting from my dad's beatings and my stepbrother's sexual abuse. James still found his way into my room, and I found myself leaving more than I was staying—that is, until Diana walked in on James.

One day as she was headed to the bathroom, she heard her son in my room and walked in, catching him touching me. She told him to leave the room and walked up to me, getting so close to my face that I could smell her disgust. "If you tell your dad, I'll tell him that it was your fault." She barely opened her mouth when she spoke. Her eyes threatened me more than my father's fist. I knew she meant every word, so I kept my mouth shut. The good thing about this was that James stopped coming into my room after that day.

Believe it or not, James became a good stepbrother as we got older. He taught me to love words and gave me a deep passion for the English language. I'm sure he was sorry for his behavior, but we never spoke about it. I was willing to forgive and he was willing to be a generous and kind brother.

Weeks after Diana found out about her son, she came into my room and threw a pair of red sandals at me. They were beautiful but too small for my feet. "These are from your mother," she said without blinking.

I looked at her, confused by what she was telling me. "My mother is dead," I told her. For a moment I thought that Diana had finally gone over the edge.

But she looked at me, shocked, then smirked and said, "She's not dead, you stupid little girl. She sent you these shoes and doesn't love you enough to know your size." At that, she walked out of the room, leaving me confused, holding on to sandals too beautiful to fit my life or my feet.

I didn't eat or sleep that night. My mother was alive. Images of my mother lying on the floor kept coming to me all night. The next morning found me sitting on my bed, holding my red sandals. The color kept reminding me of my mother's blood. I felt sad for not being able to fit into my new sandals. I felt that I was somehow letting her down. A few months later, Diana told my father that she was pregnant and that they needed my room. Her plan went a little awry when my father gave her his own surprise.

Weeks after she told my father about the pregnancy, they got into a big fight. My father drove the church bus, and I would sometimes go with him to drop off everyone. During one of those times, he told me to sit in the back and not tell anyone what I saw. He dropped off everyone except one passenger, a pretty woman with dark hair.

He kissed her, and she said something to him in Spanish and then looked back at me. He said something back to her and tried to caress her hair, but she pushed his hand off. She abruptly got up, opened the bus door, and left my father staring after her.

I never told Diana, but my father did, while fighting with her. He confessed to her on his way out, abandoning her for the woman on the bus. Diana had no choice but to send us away. She put Josiah and me on a train to New York City. We carried our clothes in brown paper bags. She asked the conductor to keep an eye on us and to make sure we got off at the proper stop. My brother and I were eight and ten, but we were so numb that we didn't react. Diana never looked back as she walked away, and we didn't cry. My little brother seemed afraid but not sad. Neither of us noticed when the train started to move because we were already gone. The movement of our own lives always seemed stronger than anything that was going on around us.

CHAPTER 14

Motown Dancing in the City

You turned my wailing into dancing;
You removed my sackcloth and clothed me with joy.
—Psalm 30:11

We arrived in New York City, holding brown paper bags while despair sat between us. Neither of us moved, fearing that we wouldn't be able to find our way back. The sound of the train played a hypnotic song that comforted our sad spirits. Dropped off at the station by Diana, we didn't understand or know where we were going. Only when the conductor announced the New York City station did we know where we were. As the conductor gestured to us, we followed him and walked out the door.

On the platform, we stood for a moment and then heard her voice. "Rebekah! Junior!" My aunt was there. We didn't have to worry anymore. Although she still looked young, there was a new sense of age on her. She ran to us as if she needed to get us before the conductor took us away. He smiled at her and released us to her. We hugged her with all the despair of people lost at sea and now found. My brother cried with relief at seeing his savior, but I looked at my aunt quietly, happy for our safety and her presence. There were lots of people running around the station, but I could clearly see God smiling at my brother and me. He was a distance away, yet close enough that I could see Him. I looked at Him, but I never smiled. The storm in me was greater than the calm He offered, and I depended on that storm to hide me.

My aunt took us to the new apartment she shared with her cousin Mildred. Back among the large buildings, I once again felt lost in their monumental presence. There were mountains upon mountains of buildings and a constant influx of people and emotions. I missed Lancaster's calmness and rolling hills of corn and wheat. Our home was ours, and the footsteps were familiar, but here in this grand oasis, strangers lived all around us. The feeling left me hollow and small.

My aunt was happy to have us with her. She kept stroking our heads and smiling at us. As we walked into the apartment, she announced our presence to all within earshot. Mildred came out and smiled at my brother and me. She had a sweet presence that reminded me of a mild brush of a feather against my face. I felt relief. My whole body started to relax. *This could be a safe place*, I thought. Mildred's daughter, Anna, appeared in the hallway, waving until Mildred moved toward us. Introductions were made, and my aunt released us to play. Within days we were best buddies. Within a week we fought like siblings. Although I didn't like the largeness of the city, I loved the family we were quickly becoming.

Mornings began with breakfast and cartoons. It took us a while to get used to their routine—the normalcy of it all seemed abnormal to us. My brother would look at me for a lead, but I didn't really know what this was supposed to look like. My aunt would hug us without reason. If we were within arm's length, we were apt to get a hug from her. I think my brother enjoyed her hugs the most because he seemed to be near her often. I would stare at his face when she hugged him, and I could see another piece of him come back. Anna and I bonded while playing dress-up and makeup. I enjoyed acting like her older sister. As each day came, a new feeling of peace surrounded my once-turbulent sea of hurt. I was able to take a bath every day, usually with my new sister. We connected so easily that entering the shower together felt normal. I never had a little sister, so Anna felt like she was mine.

Going to the bathroom was no longer a challenge, although my aunt had to give me prune juice a few times, which tasted like dirt to me. I appreciated her wanting to take care of us, so I tried to drink with little complaining.

My brother and I still hung out together, but now Anna joined us. Playing outside was an adventure. We weren't allowed to go far, but we didn't need to. There were two large buildings, side by side, so we played handball between the two buildings. Despite our age difference, my brother had a mean slam. He hit the ball with all the power his little hand had stored. I often felt the sting of his power on my face, leaving behind a round imprint. But we couldn't get angry because for the first time in our short lives, we were free to be ourselves. That sense of freedom intoxicated us into a drunken stupor of happiness and joy, which flowed even when we argued. I would yell at him for hitting me with the ball, and he would quickly say he was sorry, even when it wasn't his fault. In that place, we had the freedom to be children, and we felt unrestricted. I started to believe that God no longer wanted to punish us for being mischievous children. Mildred and my aunt Maria would watch from the living room window and cheer us on. Their cheers added to the cacophony of sound that enveloped us in the city. We thrived in its noises.

"Worldly music" was introduced to us in our new free world. Motown music was the sound that came out of every apartment. I learned that music could take me to other places, yet I could still be present. My brother and I fell in love with the Jacksons and Earth, Wind, and Fire. We began listening to them and dancing to the stimulating sounds. We would raise our hands and move our bottoms, with perpetual smiles that seemed frozen in time. It was summer, so I wore shorts and a halter top. I had never owned that type of clothing, since both my parents and Abuela were avid followers of Christ. However, my aunt and Mildred seemed to follow the God of fun, laughter, dance, and fashion, and they brought me clothes.

Every Saturday we would watch *Soul Train* and dance along with the contestants. We would form our own soul train line. Mildred and my aunt would join in, and we'd dance until our legs felt like rubber. Saturdays were my favorite time. Breakfast would be a lavish mix of pancakes or eggs, bacon, and toast, followed by endless watching of cartoons and *American Bandstand*. Then we would head out to do something fun, like going to the circus.

The aroma of popcorn and animal poop would bring forth joyful feelings of anticipation. Times like these made me think of my sad brother, John. I didn't know where he had gone and I felt selfish feeling joy while not knowing where he was. But Josiah was happy. I felt good being able to watch over him. The circus brought a whole new sense of wonder for me. Colorful images of the impossible mingled in my mind, like a genie out of her lamp. I envisioned myself flying across the audience with my arms opened wide. The music, lights, and smell took me far away to a magical place of wonder, where nothing could go wrong. In that new place, animals bowed at my command and flying was possible. I became a cliché, wanting to run away and join the circus. I told my aunt of my desire, and she smiled. After the circus, my brother and I began producing our own shows. Anna, being younger, followed our lead and became our perfect audience.

This was our perfect summer, brought about by my father's unfaithful act and Diana's need to get rid of us. We stayed until my father called. That day, our summer became cold, and the color of our fire-red sky turned an ominous gray.

CHAPTER 15

Becoming His Favorite Chosen One

I revealed myself to those who did not ask for me;
I was found by those who did not seek me.
—Isaiah 65:1

My father picked up Josiah in New York City a month before the end of our Motown summer. There was always a sense of sadness at the end of a favorite song, but we could always start the record again and end our temporary sadness. Real life doesn't have any start-overs. When happy moments end, the ring of hurt can last a lifetime.

I knew that my brother wanted to stay. We had found a new way of living, and now that we knew its taste, it was difficult to go back. My father didn't come in to say hello when he arrived. Two months of not seeing him was normal, so I didn't feel anything at his lack to see me. My aunt grabbed my brother's hand as he looked at me. I thought he was going to cry, so I smiled at him and told him, "It's okay." I was told the week before that I wouldn't be going with Josiah back to Lancaster. I was going to live with my dead mother, who was now alive. She still lived in New Jersey, and once my brother had gone, I was taken to her.

I hadn't left Little Girl Me all summer, but now I felt all the old hurts rushing back as quickly as the images passing my car window. I hadn't seen my mother since I had found her body on the bathroom floor. The fear of seeing her alive made me feel lost. When we arrived, I was taken to her front door. I felt a great deal of anxiety nestled around my heart. It seemed to beat faster than necessary. When the door finally opened, I was welcomed by a woman who looked like my mother but who had transformed into a redheaded, makeup-wearing image of what she used to be. Her smile was the only thing that seemed familiar. Then I noticed that she was wearing pants. Gone were the skirts and dresses that showed her hairy legs. Women in the Pentecostal church weren't allowed to shave, so many walked around with hairy legs and clean faces—makeup was considered the work of the devil, used to confuse men. My aunt wore makeup, but she was never an official Pentecostal woman. I had always seen her with makeup, but on my mother it seemed blasphemous. She hugged me long and hard, but my fear of dead things kept my hug light and less enthusiastic.

I don't remember how I got to my mother's house or who took me there. My mind was consumed with old hurts, and the numbness allowed me not to be in the moment. My mother introduced me to my new brother, Hector. He came to me and said hello. I felt sad for my other brothers. I never said a thing to my mother, but I wondered if she remembered her other sons. She never mentioned them, nor did I dare speak of them. Her new home was very small, with two bedrooms. I shared a room with my new brother, who seemed willing to share as long as I didn't touch his things, which was everything in the room.

My mother was so happy to see me that she hired a professional photographer to take pictures of our reunion. I could tell she was nervous. I was her daughter, but she hadn't seen me in so long that we were unfamiliar with each other. I felt a deep sadness at our strangeness. That night I closed my eyes and thought of my time with her in our large porcelain sink at our tiny kitchen in Grand Street Apartments. She would sing while she bathed me. Her hands were familiar with me, so I'd felt comfort in their touch. Yet now, in this new place, I felt lost in her company. Watching her and my new brother, Hector, I felt a pull I had never felt in my heart. They were accustomed to each other, and I was the intruder in their little family.

I started school in a new place. Everyone in the school seemed to know each other, but I was new. Because of how frequently I moved, I had become painfully shy. Making friends was something I was very unfamiliar with, so I didn't talk to anyone. During this time, I began to think of my time with my uncle Manny. He would tell me stories of Jesus, and I felt a kinship with Him, who was also unwanted.

While living with my uncle Manny, he read me stories of Jesus. He spoke of His hardships and that although He was innocent, He became despised by people who should have loved Him but instead plotted His death. My uncle also told me that my name was a Jewish name and that I should be very proud of it. "Jesus" he said, "was Jewish too." He told me how I was born in a Jewish hospital with a broken collarbone and how sad that made my parents. He said that the Jewish people were God's chosen people and that made them very special. All these stories became mixed in my head. I remembered all the times Jesus came to me and how at times I still saw Him.

I so desperately needed to be wanted and loved that I convinced myself that I was Jewish. Being Jewish meant that I was chosen by God. I knew that my family spoke Spanish, but somewhere inside of me it didn't matter because I was Jewish. Nothing else in my ten-year-old mind made sense. It wasn't that my parents didn't want me, I rationalized; it was that they couldn't handle the cost of having a daughter who was Jewish. I slowly started to allow God back into my life. Every day I walked and talked to Him. I didn't need friends in school because I had Him. He told me that I was His favorite. When I heard those words, I felt my heart flutter the way it did when I thought of Nathan.

Looking at my mother and her new son together—laughing, telling each other special secrets—didn't bother me. I was His favorite and—more important—I was Jewish and chosen.

While I lived with my mother, she worked, which meant we had to go to day care. The start of school was about a month away, and we needed to stay somewhere during the day. I hated going, but we didn't have a choice. We would play most of the time, but we would also take naps. Naptime was always difficult for me because I wanted to keep moving. After being at day care for about a week, we got used to the routine. During naptime the staff would go into another room, leaving us alone in a large room full of mats, with half of the room for boys and the other half for girls. While I lay on my back, looking at the ceiling, a girl about my age crawled over to me and whispered in my ear, "My brother likes you. He wants to talk to you." I looked over her shoulder, and behind her was her brother, smiling down at me. He was blond and tall and at least fourteen or fifteen years old. He kept smiling at me and waving. I tried to ignore him. I could see in his eyes the look that kept coming from that dark place. I rolled away from them and tried my best not to look at them.

Frustrated, he pushed his sister out of the way and lay next to me. He tried to touch me the way others had, but today was a new day, and I wasn't the same girl. I tried to keep moving, but he was bigger and stronger, and he managed to pin me down. At that moment, my mouth opened and I screamed. He tried to put his hand over my mouth, but I bit him and continued to scream until an adult came into the room. He got off before they got to me. From that day on he never bothered me. Sometimes I would see him looking at me like he had lost something, but I didn't look at him. I was God's favorite, and I didn't have to worry anymore.

After that day, I learned how to defend myself from intruders.

I felt that God had taught me that little trick. "Open thy mouth, and I shall speak." I'd heard my uncle read that verse, and now I knew its meaning. Except that God doesn't always speak our language. Sometimes He screams to move that thing that needs to move quickly. I gained a new weapon and a new identity. I was His favorite little girl.

I told someone in the day care, "God loves the broken-hearted more than those who are perfect." I believed this as truth because I didn't understand that perfect didn't exist. Bible verses gave me life and filled my life with new meaning. That's how I became Jewish and being Jewish gave me purpose that I'd never had.

CHAPTER 16

Do not fear, for I have redeemed you;
I have called you by name; you are Mine!
—Isaiah 43:1

My new identity helped me sleep better, run faster, understand my new mother and brother, and laugh with my heart wide open. I was God's child and not just any child but His favorite. My abuela and uncle told me that the Jewish people were chosen by God to be His people and because they were chosen they suffered many persecutions. I felt connected to the Jewish people and to Jesus. Being young, I couldn't explain the connection; I only understood that it made me happy. In my mind, the stories coalesced, mingling my Jewish name and birthplace into a mass of reason that could only be explained by one thing: I was Jewish!

My new little brother, Hector, would walk into the room and find me seemingly talking to myself. He would wonder about my state of mind. Talking to Jesus was as normal as two friends hanging out together. I would joke and laugh in His presence. I felt like I was living for the first time because He had chosen me and I was his favorite. Yes, I was Jewish. Although I knew that it meant my life would have struggles, it was worth it because of Him. My heart understood that when Christ chooses you, there's no greater honor. I started walking around, holding my secret like a peacock, with its feathers expanded and fearless.

My mother didn't have any of my records from my previous schools, so she registered me under her maiden name. Her hatred for my father compelled her to extinguish his name for a season. But I had a secret and nothing could change it. I was a beautiful flower plucked from a garden of millions. I walked to school and wondered if any of the children could see my secret. Every day I felt euphoric, believing that nothing could ever make me feel sad again. But children with small hands can't hold on to big dreams and my hands were very small.

Months after school started, the teacher asked everyone about their ethnicity. For months I'd known I was Jewish. That was the greatest thing about my secret; only I knew the truth of my existence. God had chosen me before my parents even knew me, so He had first dibs on me. It wasn't their fault that they couldn't keep me. It was my "Jewishness" that kept this perpetual space between them and me.

My mind was on this track of reason for a few seconds before the teacher got to me. "Okay, Rebekah, it's your turn. What is your ethnicity?"

For a moment I thought of lying, but I knew I couldn't. Being chosen meant doing the right thing, even when it's difficult. "I'm Jewish." It slipped out of my mouth like a wet gumball saturated in saliva; too slippery to stay in. *Surely*, I thought, *she can see the Jewishness in me.* She looked at me for a few moments. Her eyes seemed amused at first, but when I didn't change my answer, she asked, "What did you say?"

At that moment I knew that I shouldn't have told. It was our secret, and now everyone knew. "I'm Jewish."

She hesitated before speaking, but the words came before I was ready to receive them, "No, Rebekah, you're not Jewish. Who told you that?"

I put my head down and drank back my tears. I knew I couldn't tell her. I knew if I told her that God spoke to me and told me I was chosen that she would think I was crazy. So I said nothing.

But she wouldn't stop. "Rebekah, you're Puerto Rican. What would make you say such a silly thing?"

The gumball was replaced by a wad of sand, and I couldn't speak. The other children laughed as I sat looking down at my desk. All day my mind couldn't wrap itself around the truth and fought to find a solution. I finally reasoned with myself: *What does this teacher know about me?* I ran home with her words biting the backs of my heels, desperately avoiding its imprint.

I found my mother in her bedroom, folding clothes. She looked tired and helpless, and I still couldn't get used to her red hair. Maybe she couldn't remember my Jewishness. Maybe she couldn't remember because she had been gone for so long that her memory of me had faded with the memory of my last name. I didn't see her look up. I had begun to turn away, believing that maybe this wasn't such a good idea. I was going to talk to God—He would know what to do—but before I could leave, she looked up and said, "Rebekah, are you okay?" I turned and looked at her. She smiled and gestured for me to come over. "How was school today?"

I knew then that I had to tell her. "It was okay."

"Really? You look a little sad. What's wrong?"

Once again I knew I couldn't lie. "The teacher said that I wasn't Jewish."

My mother stopped what she was doing and looked at me as if she hadn't heard me. "Who's not Jewish?"

"She said that I'm not Jewish, but I am, right?"

Without taking a breath, she answered, "No, you're not Jewish! Why would you believe that?"

My heart stopped for a millisecond, and when it restarted, it sounded and felt different. Another piece had broken off, and I didn't have anywhere to go with it. She kept talking and asking questions, but I couldn't talk. The familiar clump of sand came back. I choked and ran out the room.

I ran outside and down the street. We lived near the center of town, so cars were coming and going, unaware of my heartbreak. I wasn't Jewish. The sun was shining. Its warmth warmed my skin, but my heart felt as cold as winter snow. I found a tree in a neighbor's yard and sat under it. *What is a Puerto Rican, and are they chosen?* Tears streamed down my face. I was a nothing in a nobody's place. I wasn't one of His chosen people. I was no one's chosen. I sat and cried endless tears. I stayed under that tree until the sun had done its time and began to descend from a long day's work. Streaks of fire crossed the sky, orange and yellow burning away what was left of the blue, leaving behind dark ashes that surrounded my heart, leaving me feeling empty and forgotten.

CHAPTER 17

Where, Oh Where?

Now faith is the assurance of things hoped for,
the conviction of things not seen.
—Hebrew 11:1

I opened my eyes and listened to the hum of the engine. We'd been in the air for about an hour, and I couldn't stop the tears from flowing. Looking down at my checkered pants, I stared at the colors that joined together in perfect harmony and wondered why my life couldn't look the same. I thought of my abuela and knew that these pants would be a point of contention for her. "Pants are a sin. They are made for men to wear, not women," she would say. I could hear my abuela's voice, full of disappointment and judgment, and at that moment I wished my mom had given me a dress. My anxiety rose at the thought of seeing her, so I closed my eyes and listened to the sound of the engines. I tried to will myself back to sleep, but my mind wouldn't allow it.

Money was always a problem for my mother, and getting child support from my father wasn't an option. One evening, while she struggled with bills once again, she picked up the phone and called my abuela. She looked around to make sure I wasn't in the room, but she had forgotten how small the apartment was and how easily the walls gave up its security. She asked Abuela if I could live with her. I couldn't hear what Abuela said, but now the answer was apparent.

At the airport, my mother cried. "Sorry, Rebekah, but I just can't afford you. Abuela said she would take you for a little while. Maybe I can get a better job and get you back, okay?" I cried without regret. I wanted her to see all the tears that I had held back when I thought she was dead. Now that she was alive, I wanted her to know how much I loved her. Maybe if I didn't hold anything back, she would keep me. Maybe her heart would hurt as much as mine and she wouldn't send me away. It didn't work. Sitting with my eyes closed, I could see her face twisted in both sadness and regret. I was told that Abuela had moved to Puerto Rico for a better life. I wondered if she had left to get away from the craziness of life in New York. Her sons were still on drugs, and I was still homeless. I usually felt sorry for Abuela, but in that moment I only felt sorry for myself. Who would want me? I saw the way my mom looked at Hector. Why couldn't she look at me that way?

After my realization that I wasn't Jewish, I felt devastated for a while. I walked around in a daze, wondering why God had allowed me to believe such a fable. Then I understood; I was His favorite. He loved me because I was like Him. He was also unwanted by His own people. My parents understood His Jewishness from an ethnic point of view, but I understood Him from a place in my heart. Only I could understand because we were connected, heart to heart, by brokenness.

The stewardess came and asked if I wanted something to eat. "No," I said. She noticed that I had been crying, so she sat in the empty seat next to me and said, "You're going to love Puerto Rico. It is warm and the sky is very blue. But the best thing about it is the beach. You could go swimming as much as you want in Puerto Rico because the weather is beautiful all year round. Isn't that good?" She looked at me as if she had given me a special gift. What she didn't know was that Abuela didn't believe in bathing suits either, so she wouldn't let me go to the beach.

I looked at the stewardess and smiled. As she walked away, I wondered about this new place. Would it look like New Jersey, with its mix of tall buildings and small homes, or like New York, with its tall buildings and wall-to-wall cars, or Lancaster, Pennsylvania, with its rolling hills full of corn, cows, and buggies? I stayed on that thought until I fell asleep.

The stewardess woke me when we arrived. She took my hand and walked me out of the door. As soon as we were outside, I knew that this place was not like any other. The heat was the first to welcome me. It hit my nostrils and it took a couple of seconds for me to begin breathing normally again. Then I saw them. Tall and elegant, like models with long legs. The breeze was warm, and the tops of these odd trees swayed back and forth. They seem to wave and I dared to believe that God was using them to welcome me. I smiled and looked up at the lady whose hand I was still holding. "What are they?" I asked her. I wanted to know the names of the trees that were so gracious in welcoming me to this new, strange place.

"Palm trees. You like them?"

I nodded my head, and she nodded hers as we walked. I looked ahead; I noticed Abuela standing near a desk. She was talking to someone across from her. As I got closer, I called out, "Hi, Abuela!"

She smiled and waved at me. Then she noticed my pants. Her face changed a bit, but she kept smiling. The lady said hello to my abuela and told her that I was a very good girl. I waved at the lady, and she bent down and hugged me. My abuela thanked her, and we were off. Abuela started asking about the airplane ride. She never mentioned my pants, which I was thankful for. That helped me relax. As we entered the car, I noticed more palm trees. *This is a weird place*, I thought. *Why can't trees afford more branches, and why do the trunks grow tall and slim?* I wondered if they were trying to reach God, and I felt a deeper connection with their persistence to reach Him.

Life with Abuela in Puerto Rico was very different from New York. She spoke Spanish a lot, and it was difficult keeping up with her. She would forget that I didn't understand Spanish and would go on speaking without stopping to think that I didn't comprehend her. Here, she had a white poodle called Whitey. She loved that dog as much as she loved me (at least, that's what I believed at the time). I enjoyed having the dog around since Abuela was gone so often. After a few weeks had passed, she decided to enroll me in school, but things were different here. I needed to learn Spanish. Classes were divided into morning and afternoon classes because of the weather.

I was put in first grade in the morning in an effort to teach me Spanish. Then in the afternoon I would go to school to the fifth-grade and sit with children I didn't understand. I felt embarrassed, ashamed, and stupid. So I began to act out and became the class clown. In frustration, the fifth-grade teacher threw erasers at me. The principal called Abuela, and when she arrived she was aggravated. She owned her own business and getting away from it meant she had less money to take care of her household. She was still the main provider and needed to work. Although she might not have meant to show it, I felt her resentment, so I began to resent her too.

The thought of my childish resentment toward her makes me feel sad, even today. She was doing her best, but I couldn't understand because I was consumed with self-pity and the hurt of feeling rejected. I lasted with Abuela for about four months. While there, I became more introverted and refused to love Abuela's God. Her God seemed harsh and small, especially since He couldn't love a little girl who wore pants. Abuela took all my pants and converted them into skirts, hoping that her God would accept me. She tried everything within her power to change my view of her God. She tried to explain why pants had the power to send me into the fiery furnace. I wished that I could have explained to Abuela that I already lived there, no matter what I wore. I rejected her skirt-wearing religion. She became angry at my refusal to believe. She needed peace, and I was too full of rebellion to give in to her need.

On the plane coming back, I didn't know where I was going. I looked out the window and wondered if anyone would notice if I jumped out. I looked around to see if there was a way out, but I couldn't find any, so I sat listening to the hum of the engine and wondered if home was a place not meant for me. I fell asleep with this thought and awoke to find myself back in New York City, suffering from a great case of hopelessness. At that moment, I wondered if God would reconsider having me as one of His chosen. The weight of His call seemed too much for me to bear.

During this time was when my uncle Bobby was killed. My abuela was one of the first people to find him hanging in a small wooden shack in Puerto Rico. I didn't realize what my abuela was going through. Once again, I was too involved with myself to look beyond to anyone else's hurt. During my short time with Abuela, she always tried to make my favorite food. A tuna fish sandwich, which she made triple-decker style, and a tall glass of soda was her way of showing me love at a time when she carried great pain. This would be the last time I would live with my abuela. I saw her briefly as a teenager when I went to Puerto Rico to visit her with my aunt during Hurricane David. The last time I saw her was when I had my daughters, and we took a picture together—Abuela, my mother, and me—three generations. She died about a year after that picture was taken. It was six o'clock in the morning, and she was driving to her business when she had a massive heart attack in her car. She died the way she lived—moving.

CHAPTER 18

Hope on False Deliverance Can't Save

A horse is a vain hope for deliverance;
despite all it's great strength it cannot save.
—Psalm 33:17

My heart was in a dull place when I arrived in New York City. When you understand that nothing is for you and everything is against you, the heart becomes dismal and rejects feeling what the mind so clearly understands but refuses to believe.

Abuela had seemed changed with the heat and the palm trees. She made sure that I had what I needed, but our emotional distance created a deep heartache for a love that never was satisfied. Her love for me was never in question, but I wanted her to stop and see me. Whenever I think of my abuela, she was always in perpetual movement. My mind went to a sad place while in Puerto Rico. I didn't feel wanted by anyone, and even Abuela was so busy that I became an inconvenience.

I came back to live with my aunt in New York City. She was now married and renting a one-room apartment. I slept in the living room, which consisted of a sofa bed and dining room table. Every morning my new uncle would sit and talk to me. He began cooking my favorite foods and showing me attention I hadn't experienced in a long time. I loved music, so we began to share our passion for music. He loved Latin music and would play Tito Puente, Willie Colon, and Celia Cruz. He began teaching me how to dance salsa. I found that I was a natural, and my hips moved with the ease of a hula dancer. Dancing together in the middle of the living room for what seemed like hours gave my mind rest from the negativity, and I slowly began to find joy again.

My aunt was proud of my immediate attachment to her new husband, and once again I dared to believe that a family was forming. Almost every Saturday we would go to his family's apartment, where they made up songs using bongos and maracas, while singing lyrics of pain and joy. Those of us who couldn't make music would dance to the music in a way that would reflect what they were feeling. We would go and dance for hours. My uncle would laugh and talk about how great a partner I was. He had the ability to speak into my dry places and produce springs of new hope. People would gather around us and wonder how such a young girl could dance with such womanly sophistication.

My uncle was about six foot one, with dark skin. When he smiled the sun couldn't compete with the warmth his smile gave. Some may had mistaken him for being African American, but he was pure Puerto Rican. His family came to New York from Puerto Rico, and he was proud of his heritage. He seemed almost perfect to me, except for his one flaw. His smile had the power to seduce women, and soon I noticed his willingness to use it. I tried to tell my aunt, but she was newly married, and he convinced her that I was only seeing things. He forgave me this little indiscretion because he thought of me as a naive child. He didn't know all that I had seen.

I also forgave my uncle of this flaw. I loved him so much that I wanted to believe that he was perfect. I looked away when I saw his eyes become hypnotized as he watched the movements of another woman's hips. I would grab his arm and sway him back to me. I didn't want him to look at other women that way. Memories of my dad looking at women in the same way came back to me. I could see the sadness and disappointment in my mother's eyes, knowing that her husband didn't see her as enough. I never wanted my aunt feeling that way, but I had no control to stop him.

Soon my aunt began to call him vulgar names. I wondered if she was starting to see his power too. He didn't seem to hear her, so her voice became louder, and the names became uglier. I chose not to look at what was going on between them. He was my uncle, and he cared about me. I would draw and write, and he would make an effort to listen and see what was going on in the depths of my heart. He seemed to see me and never walked by me without recognizing me.

He started noticing that I was home alone a lot, so he began taking me to work with him at the World Trade Center. My uncle was a very gregarious man. He attracted people to him. People he worked with would come over and ask me to do little odd jobs for them. They enjoyed my uncle's presence and would do anything to make his niece feel as special as he made them feel. I felt wanted and appreciated, and for the first time in my life I had purpose. When I began school, I wanted to do my best because I wanted him to be proud of me. I wanted my new uncle to think of me as smart. After a while he began to call me "baby girl," and although I was about thirteen years old, the nickname made me feel small and protected. I hadn't felt this way since spending time with my father-uncle Bobby, and I liked the feeling.

Music became my solace. I would sit on the sofa and listen for hours. It didn't matter if it was Latin or Motown; I would be engrossed in singing, and my soul would go to hopeful places. I would feel the music deep inside and be moved to emotion by the words. I wondered what kind of love moved people to write and sing and bare their souls in such a raw way. Rhythm gave them permission to express themselves when conversation wasn't comfortable. When no one was home, I would blast the music and dance until beads of sweat rolled down my back. I was alone a lot after school started. I didn't like my school, so making friends seemed impossible. I became friends with Gladys Knight and the Pips, Willie Colon, and Michael Jackson. My uncle opened my mind to a new world. I felt totally at home with their pain and heartache. Unfortunately, he also opened my heart to death. Dying is never easy when love is still raw and holding on to blue pieces.

CHAPTER 19

God Loved David B.

Oh, that I might have my request,
that God would grant what I hope for.

—Job 6:8

The school bell rang. It felt as if it was beating against the sides of my brain. I couldn't stop my anxiety. The halls, bathrooms, and classrooms were jammed with kids. I felt lost in a building full of hormones. While looking for my homeroom, I could feel eyes on me. I was the new girl, and the pack wanted to know her scent. When I finally found my homeroom, I sat in the first desk I could find.

"David, can you please sit down?" the teacher said as the rest of the class arrived. I could feel the person behind me sit and stare at the back of my head. I tried my best not to look, so I stared ahead at the teacher, hoping the pressure I felt behind me would stop. "Okay, settle down, everyone. Let's take attendance." He began to read the names one by one, and each student, one by one, said, "Here." Lost in thought mixed with anxiety, I didn't hear my name called. "Rebekah?"

"Oh yeah, here," I said. Some students laughed, and others rolled their eyes. I could almost hear their thoughts: *New girl doesn't even know her own name. She's probably stupid."* And at that moment I felt both stupid and visible. I wanted to shrink and become so small that no one would notice me.

"Hey," the voice said from behind me.

Oh boy, I thought, *it's that David guy the teacher was talking to.*

"Hey, don't worry about it. Most of these people are a bunch of dummies anyway. They come here because no one else wants them around, not even their own parents." And that's how David B. introduced himself to me.

Weeks after I started school, I noticed something about my new friend David—he had a way with the girls. He was about five foot eight; tall for an eighth-grader. His olive skin was perfect. I wanted to touch it—and so did every girl in school. When he smiled, his perfect teeth were accentuated by his full lips; it reminded me of my uncle Tony's smile. He had dark hair that would end up around his eyes when he laughed, and he laughed a lot. In class, the teacher often told him to settle down. He was the most handsome boy I had ever seen, but I was afraid to look into his eyes. Whenever he spoke to me, I would look at his chest, his arms, his lips, even his hair, but his eyes felt dangerous to me.

I did well in school. I loved my uncle and wanted to show him that I was worthy of his love, so I worked hard at getting good grades. Although that won me accolades at home, in school it earned me ridicule. Kids started bullying me and calling me teacher's pet. Teachers would compliment me, which made me feel uncomfortable but I couldn't stop working hard. So I began cutting school. It wasn't difficult to catch up because I would make sure to read ahead or work all weekend. David started noticing me too. He would smile at me as we walked down the hall. Girls and boys of all ages would stand around him. He was a good athlete, involved in basketball and he played a mean game of handball. The school had handball courts. In the morning, while we waited for the doors to open, many would play with the small, tight blue ball.

It was first come, first serve, but when David came, he was

always given a court. I was the dork sitting on the stairs at the side of the playground, reading. Reading could usually take me out of this place, but I became distracted by David. He would play handball as if his life depended on his winning. Rarely did he lose, but when he did, he was gracious although his face seemed strained, as if he had lost more than he had bargained.

Girls were always near him, trying to get his attention. He ignored them when he played, but once he was done they would surround him like his personal harem. Girls often fought over him, and their fights were vicious. He never watched them fight but walked away, leaving them alone in their foolish act of empty adornment.

I felt an odd connection with David B. I wasn't like the girls who wanted just a simple touch of his hand or a look of desire from him. Something about him connected with me. I knew if I looked into his eyes I would see it, and that produced fear in me. At times I would catch him watching me. Walking down the hall, I would look up, and there he would be. He never bothered me but seemed to be a constant presence whenever I was in school. When I did go to school, I would walk with my head down and try not to make eye contact with anyone. Every once in a while when I would return, David would ask me, "Where were you?"

I never answered him. I was stuck between wanting to do well for my uncle and the fear of getting beaten up. I had seen girls cut each other in the face with blades and boys beat each other with bats. I knew that sooner or later that would be my fate, so I did everything I could to stay out of everyone's way. Then one day a teacher handed me my paper with an A on it and did something to seal my fate—he told everyone about my grade. It seemed that I was the only one who had passed, and his frustration didn't allow his mouth to stay shut. I was stunned. I heard the whispers and knew today was going to be the day. But how? The fear of a blade cutting my face made my knees want to buckle. The bell rang, signaling it was time to go to the next class.

I got up, grabbed my books, and began walking toward the door. I was so focused on the door that I didn't realize that a boy had come up behind me. He grabbed my butt and slapped it hard; everyone heard and saw what he did. As they laughed, I lost my mind. I dropped all my books except the science book, which was the thickest book I had. I turned, holding my book like a weapon. The boy was too busy looking around with satisfaction, so when I hit him on the head he wasn't expecting it. All the frustration and torment of my past came out in that moment. The boy went down, and I was on top of him, screaming, "Don't"—*bang*—"you"—*bang*—"ever"—*bang*—"touch me"—*bang*—"again!" *Bang, bang, bang, bang.* I kept beating him until David grabbed me and stopped me.

He wasn't in this class, so he didn't know the reason I was beating the guy. He grabbed me by the waist and called to me. "Rebekah, it's okay. I think he got the message."

I was filled with so much rage that even when David grabbed me, I kept swinging. He continued hugging me until I felt all the rage melt, and all that was left was grief. David held me as I cried. The kids respected and even feared David, so no one dared say a word. The crowd slowly dispersed until it was just him and me. When we were alone, he leaned toward my ear and whispered, "I know how you feel. I understand you, and it's okay. I won't let them hurt you."

After that day, no one bothered me. No one called my home. Not even the teachers mentioned the incident, and school went on as if nothing had ever happened. There was only one difference: David's presence in my life became magnified. I kept missing school, which eventually caught up to me. My aunt decided to send me back to my mother because I wouldn't stop cutting school, no matter what they said. My uncle tried to speak to me, but I didn't want him to know that I feared being in school. Although no one bothered me, I could see the looks, especially from girls who thought that David B. was theirs. He wouldn't stop looking after me, and they couldn't understand his connection with me. I couldn't explain it myself. I just knew that somehow we were connected.

When my aunt said that I would be going back to New Jersey in two weeks, I was both glad and sad. I wanted out of this crazy environment, but I knew that I would never see David B. again. The day I found out, I couldn't stop thinking about him. I went to school the next day with the desire to speak to him. When I saw him, I couldn't talk. I stared into his eyes and felt helpless. We stared at each other with a deep understanding I had never felt with anyone. He smiled at me, but all I could do was look at him. I knew that look of despair and sense of hopelessness. Within moments, his pain overwhelmed me, and I looked away. I felt that I was looking deeply into a mirror, and I rarely looked at myself in the mirror. That was the last time I saw David B. There are some people who stay with you, not because of anything they've done but because you know that if you were to open them up, they would look just like you on the inside, and with that realization, the world doesn't seem so lonely.

Two days before I was to leave, I was told the news of why David hadn't been in school for over a week. His father had killed him, beaten him to death. I was told that his father beat him often, but this time David fought back. This time he lost. I cried for David, not because he was dead but because he had left me behind. I left school that day, walked home, and sat out in the hallway of our apartment building and prayed for David. I asked Jesus why He loved David B. more than me, but He never answered.

CHAPTER 20

Misery Doesn't Always Love Company

Record my misery; list my tears on your scroll
are they not in your records?

—Psalm 56:8

A fearlessness rose within me after David's death. Pinocchio dreams are hard to hold on to when hope is left in tears too long. Hope begins to warp and buckle in the middle. I no longer cared if anyone came for me, so I began to believe that I was invincible—or maybe it was more like invisible.

Living with my mother again was like living in a war zone that was constantly on red alert. While she worked, I took care of my brother Hector, which meant I was always at his mercy. I thought he was spoiled, and taunting me became his favorite form of entertainment. He knew that I had many dislikes about myself, but my greatest one was my nose. It was wide and turned up slightly at the end. I felt that when people looked at me, my nose was all they could see. When Hector and I were alone, he would follow me, chanting, "Big nose, big nose, Rebekah has a big nose." No matter how loudly I yelled at him, he wouldn't stop. He was relentless. The apartment we lived in was small, and we could reach any part of it with a couple of steps. His chant reverberated against the walls, and the sound of it began to wear me down. When I would tell my mother, she would look at me as if I were offending her. She had little time, and she didn't want to spend it refereeing Hector and me. I realized that I was on my own.

As Hector's pestering reached a new level, I reached a level of my own. Beating him mercilessly became my outlet. He complained to my mother, and she beat me. The cycle would have been ridiculous if it hadn't been so pathetic. Then she would yell at me, telling me that I needed to stop fighting with my "brother." The words "your brother" produced the same feeling in me as the sound of someone scratching a chalkboard.

Then Hector would return and begin his torment again with what seemed to be my mother's blessing. This may seem a small point, but I was already in a state of self-hate. I didn't understand why no one wanted me; I felt dispensable. Hector was as lonely as I was, but I was young, and being reasonable was lost on me. We were stuck in a small apartment together every day after school. There were moments when I tried to do normal things with him, like throwing a football or a baseball, but we always found our way back to his teasing me and my beating him. As our cycles worsened, I began locking myself in the tiny bathroom. Living in a two-bedroom apartment meant that I shared a room with Hector, so the only privacy I had was the bathroom. In that tiny space I got relief—found at the edge of a blade; sharp, shiny, and cold.

I discovered my mother's shaving blade had power. The razor was the type that was opened by twisting it, and then a thin, sharp blade, simple and innocuous, was inserted. The blade was so sharp that I cut myself the first time I touched it. Looking at my blood made me feel better. I began cutting myself lightly on the arm and watched my blood spill, feeling euphoric and invincible. In those moments, I held my life in my own hands, and no one could tell me what to do with it. I thought of David B. and wondered how he felt when he knew that he was going to die. I started glamorizing death. It became perverted in my mind as an option out of my current situation. I would sit in the bathroom, looking at the blade and imagining my death. Suicide became my companion. I didn't know its name, but I knew that when the thought came to me, it created a great amount of comfort. It felt like a promise of something better when everything looked hopeless and lost. I thought about all the places I'd been and all the people I had lived with, and I wondered if they would come to my funeral. Would they feel any remorse at my death? Weeping in my distorted reality, suicide said that no one would really care. Visions of my death began to torment me even more than Hector. The sense that no one wanted me was so unbearable that I began dreaming that death was coming for me.

Then the day came when I readied myself for suicide, with blade in hand, until a voice spoke my brothers' names into me. An image played in my mind. I saw that if I killed myself, I wouldn't see them again, and the pain of not seeing them again was greater than the pain of not being wanted. My heart had tried to forget them because I hadn't seen them in years. I would ask my mother about them, but she never had an answer for me, so I turned my rage against her.

Suicide pursued me. Although I had given up the moment, the moment wasn't giving up on me. I still cut myself with a blade, but now I had learned how to use words to cut my mother. She would come home tired, and I would pursue her with questions about my brothers. Why weren't they with us? Why didn't she want them? Everything she said sounded like an excuse to me. I never saw her tired eyes or the look of feeling overwhelmed. Anger blinded me against seeing anyone else's pain, especially hers. I had seen too much and felt too much and knew that Pinocchio was a fairy tale. No one was capable of saving me.

I became belligerent toward her, and I didn't care what came out of my mouth. I would yell at her, telling her that she didn't love my brothers, only her spoiled son Hector. I told her that she didn't deserve having us. I became a source of torment for her. I started to leave Little Girl Me again and go into a black hole where nothing could reach me. My mother had no faith; God was absent from her life, so He became absent in mine. I thought about death, hate, and sadness all the time. I wanted my mother to fight for me, but she couldn't do for me what she wasn't willing to do for herself. She worked all the time and felt fatigued and helpless. She needed me to take care of myself because emotionally, she was running on low too.

I blamed Hector and hated him for taking my mother's affection away from my brothers and me. I felt that we were first and that he was an intruder. She beat me with a belt to try to control me. Her beatings were nothing compared to my father's. The only pain I felt came from deep in my heart. My tears were never about what she was doing but for what she wasn't doing. I thought of my brothers with a stepmother who didn't love them and now a mother who had forgotten them. All I wanted was to see them again, and the thought made me oppose her for them.

Something inside of me started to fall apart. I would look at my mother as if she were an imposter. My mother had actually died in the bathroom at Grant Street Apartments. She would never allow anyone to hurt me, and she would never beat me. Yes, she was gone, as was any hope of finding her again. I didn't understand her replacement any more than I understood Hector. My anger and bitterness were reflected in my mother's constant yelling. She yelled about the house, the food, lack of money, and my tantrums. Anything seemed to set her off. She could yell for what seemed like hours. Then I would blow and tell her to be quiet. On days when I sensed she was about to lose her mind, I tiptoed around her as if walking in a minefield. I feared she'd explode and leave me emotionally in pieces. She no doubt felt the same way about me because we rarely came near each other.

CHAPTER 21

Losing Weight While Losing My Mind

I can count all my bones;
people stare and gloat over me.
—Psalm 22:17

I lived with my mother for about three months, until the school year was over. I rebelled, and she didn't know what to do with a girl who needed a mother. My father picked me up, but my mind was gone during the drive back to Lancaster, Pennsylvania. My thoughts were stuck with my mother and my brother. I could hear Hector mocking me as I left, although in reality he hadn't said a thing. Actually, while my dad was pulling away, I looked back at Hector. He looked sad as he stood alone on the sidewalk, but in my own darkness, I heard him mocking and taunting me. "Na-na-na-na-na! She's my mom, not yours." When he waved, I looked away, lost in my own hurt and unwilling to see his. I didn't want to grasp what my heart already understood—she loved him more than me, more than all of us.

The drive back was long, and my emotions volleyed between excitement at seeing my brothers and sadness at knowing that my real mother had died. I was consumed with thoughts of her bathing us in the kitchen in the large porcelain sink. She would sing, and her voice soothed whatever unrest my father left behind. Closing my eyes I could see my brother Josiah, small and helpless, standing near her. In her presence, we knew that no matter how angry our father became she would always cover us with her protection, wrapped in love and warmth. I felt the coolness of the sink on my backside and the warmth of the water. Like the taste of sweet and salty, it made no sense in thought but with experience formed a perfect unity. I stayed in that place as the miles passed, and before I knew it we were there. As my father parked, I noticed that we were in a new neighborhood. Gone were the small brick homes standing at attention. Now the homes had no uniformity or unity in spirit. The new home was larger, but its gray stone exterior seemed cold and lacked the pride of the warm brick. Lost in thought for a couple of seconds, I was awakened when I saw my brothers from the corner of my eye. They stood outside, waving and calling out to me. My older brother, John, was much taller, and his eyes looked older than his age. Josiah also had grown taller but was very thin—abnormally thin—and he moved like an old man. "Dad, what's wrong with Josiah? He looks sick." I could feel the tears readying themselves as I tried to hold them back.

"Oh, he was sick. He had to go to the hospital and have another operation, but he's okay now," my dad said.

Another operation? I didn't even know about the first one. I got out of the car as quickly as I could. Gone were my earlier thoughts; my brothers needed me. I hugged Josiah long and tight. I could tell he felt a little embarrassed by my emotions, but I couldn't stop myself. John reached over and hugged me, his eyes understanding the moment.

We walked into the living room, with its wall-to-wall red-white-and-blue shag rug and brown-and-orange wallpaper. The stairs that led to the second floor were covered with rug samples of different colors and textures that my father had stapled in place. My room was larger than before, and the twin bed had been replaced with a full-size bed and a large wardrobe dresser, but it was as chaotic in color and style as the rest of the house. Decorated with wallpaper that celebrated America's bicentennial and with a red-white-and-blue shag rug, the room looked frozen in patriotism. My father had promised to fix the house when they moved in two years earlier, but his constant procrastination kept the house in a perpetual 1950s-era motif. The kitchen and bathroom were avocado green and goldenrod yellow. We had only one small bathroom for five boys, two adults, and me. The avocado-green bathtub had gold-framed sliding doors. The sink was the perfect size for a nine-year-old child, so when we washed our faces or brushed our teeth, puddles of water would form below the sink. The white toilet was new, and it looked as out of place as I felt. The floor and walls were a muted green-yellow, which felt like a cocoon of mold whenever I was in the bathroom.

My brothers explained that my father had bought all the rugs and wallpaper at a going-out-of-business sale, hence the bicentennial theme. And for his support, the business gave him rug samples. I guess that explained the patchwork on the stairs. Living in Lancaster County, quilts were a part of our culture and could be seen everywhere. Maybe he thought that using the same concept of a patchwork quilt on the stairs would be a good thing; it wasn't. It only added to the chaos in the home. The chaotic décor was reflected in our chaotic family, and I instantly knew why this was home.

My father's truck-driving schedule kept him gone for most of the day. Diana had to take care of us, and after four years she still struggled and would often fall off the edge. However, my brothers were older and now were immune to her rages. I was immune to her too but for different reasons, I had learned not to care. I was courteous but had little to offer her, other than my silence, which I gave freely. While I was away, Diana and my father had another son together. They named him Edwin, which later was shortened to Ed. Ed was a quiet little boy with a quiet spirit. When we were together, he would get lost in our energy, and we would barely see him. He was always trying to do good, which only made me stay away from him. He could afford the luxury of good because he had his mother's protection, but my brothers and I only had each other.

Josiah and I started hanging out together again. I was pleased to show him how to dance salsa and the merengue the way my uncle had shown me. Listening to the radio wasn't permitted, but as I told Josiah about salsa music, we found ways to use my father's radio. His radio was located in living room, and while everyone was out of the house, we would turn it on to salsa music. Smack in the middle of the war zone, I taught my brother how to dance, swishing my hips from side to side, fearless and free. He was stiff at first, and we would laugh at his uneasiness.

"Look—do it like this," I'd tell him. Throwing up my arms, I'd exaggerate the movements of my hips and feet. "One, two, three. One, two, three. That's how you move your feet. Now add your hips." Eventually he caught on, and we would dance all around the living room, laughing and pretending we had reasons to dance.

When we couldn't find the music, we would make up our own. I loved the way my uncle and his family worked together to make their own music, so we began do the same. The living room table became our bongos, and the music we had in our heads tried its best to come out. Our favorite became *"El maltillo, el maltillo, que pone cosas* together, forever. You, me. Together, forever." We sang in Spanglish because my brother didn't understand any Spanish, and this way, I figured, he could learn a little. Translation: "The hammer, the hammer that puts things together, forever. You, me. Together, forever." My brother was naturally gifted at playing any instrument, so he managed to make the tables sound good. I would get up and dance the way my uncle Tony had taught me. We would laugh at our little music production. The fact that we were dancing in the middle of a war zone never stopped us from laughing too loud.

Diana still hoarded food in her room. She would come in with shopping bags and take some upstairs to her padlocked room. Whenever we took anything out of the refrigerator, she would watch us. Food became a commodity that she controlled and gave little of. I was angry with her for withholding food and decided to stop eating. I was tired of people telling me what to do and when to do it. They dictated where I would go, when I would go, and with whom I would go, but they couldn't control whether I ate or not.

No one really noticed at first. During dinner we all sat together and prayed, but after we prayed, it was a free-for-all. I would put little on my plate, and then give whatever I didn't eat to my brothers. The boys ate as if it were their last meal. With the lack of available food, they made sure that they ate until they were full, so no one noticed when I began eating less. About a month into my self-imposed fast, Josiah came into my room.

"Rebekah, you're getting too skinny." I was lying in bed, wearing a green-striped dress that my aunt had given me when I was younger, and now I was able to fit into it again. "You need to eat." As he said these words he began to count my ribs.

I laughed and said, "Stop it. I'm okay. I like being skinny, and that way Diana can keep her stupid food." My brother looked at me with sadness in his eyes. I hated when people looked at me that way, so I told him to get out of my room and stop being silly. I tried to sound lighthearted, but as he left, he looked at me with the same sad eyes that Ruth and Manny had, so I pushed him out and closed the door.

Later that evening, I went into the bathroom and pulled out an old scale to weigh myself. When I first started my fast, I weighed 130 pounds. I was now eighty-nine pounds. I had lost forty pounds in a month. The loss made me smile. For once I had control, and no one was going to tell me what to do—at least, that's what I believed at that time, and the thought made me happy.

CHAPTER 22

The Heart of a Fatherless Gang

The heart of the wise inclines to the right,
but the heart of the fool to the left.
—Ecclesiastes 10:2

One evening my father noticed that I had lost a lot of weight. He told me to start eating. As I sat staring at the food, he decided that I wasn't moving fast enough, and he hit me over the head with the plate of food. I suppose he believed that direct intervention with the problem was the best therapy, and I guess it worked because I started eating after that. I didn't want his violent attention, so I began to eat everything, including my emotions. By the time he sent me back to my mother's, I was back to my normal overweight body. I wasn't told why I was going back this time. I believe everyone was running out of excuses and decided that I had heard them all. I wanted to stay with my brothers, but that was never my option. A worn-out sorrow came for me that morning, but I knew that complaining would only anger my father, so I left in silence.

Back in Paterson, I noticed that my mother had once again moved to a new location. The neighborhood was lined with trees, and children flowed in and out of the homes around us. For the first time in my life, children my age lived around me, and having friends became an option I'd never had before. Lillian, Sandra, Amy, and Sabrina instantly became my friends. I met them on my first day of school. We walked to school together almost every day. I felt content although I missed my brothers. I knew that mourning them never helped, so I allowed myself to feel happy. My new friends handed me acceptance like a gift that I never deserved but so desperately needed. For the first time, I was able to have sleepovers. We would put on my mother's makeup and style our hair. Life felt like a dream, and I couldn't believe it was happening to me. My aunt sent me stylish clothes and I found that I enjoyed putting outfits together. Going to school and showing off my clothing added to my euphoria as people began to compliment me and copy my style. To my amazement, I quickly became popular at school. Everyone knew my name. I no longer was invisible. After school we would go home, change clothes, and go back out the door to hang out. Running around the neighborhood and getting into innocent trouble made me feel like a normal girl. My mother worked long hours and was rarely home when we got home from school. I was still responsible for my little brother, but he had grown up in the summer we were away from each other. He found his own friends and ways to entertain himself. My mother worked most Saturdays, so my house became the hangout. Saturday was our favorite day, especially when we noticed a new family moving into our neighborhood. Sabrina was the first to see the boys. They were about our age, and of course she thought they were cute.

Oliver and Chris were brothers but had different fathers. They were as different as left and right. Oliver was tall with dark skin and straight dark hair. Chris was short with light skin and curly dark hair. Oliver was good and honest and always put others first. He loved his mother and sister and was their constant protector.

Although Chris loved his family, he seemed stuck on himself. Everything he did was self-motivated and left little room for anyone else. Oliver had the looks, but most of the girls overlooked him.

He was too good, and there was no spirit of adventure in him. His brother was the bad boy, and the girls all wanted to tame him. He treated girls with cavalier intentions, but their desire to domesticate him kept them hungry for him. He smoked, drank, and cursed better than any man twice his age. He had rugged good looks and walked into a room with a swagger. His presence made girls want to bathe in his rebellion, and many made fools of themselves trying.

Oliver was kind and steadfast, and the smoothness of his demeanor made him appear boring. In our neighborhood, there were more girls than boys, so when Oliver and Chris moved in we all noticed. It took us a week before we found the courage to introduce ourselves—well, we did it in a sideways manner because meeting them head-on would have been too forward.

Our girl gang consisted of five girls who constantly hung out together. We decided that walking past the "new boys" would get their attention. We waited until we saw them sitting on their front steps and made our move. We walked slowly and pretended to be engrossed in a private conversation.

"Hey there, how you doing?" Chris saw us first and couldn't resist calling to us. We were like fresh bait for him, and he was instantly hooked. "Do you live around here?"

We looked at each other and, in typical girl fashion, giggled. "Yup, we live around here," I said. "Why? What do you want?" I wanted him to know that we weren't easy. I was tough and cared very little about boys, so I kept walking as I answered him.

"Hey, wait a minute! Where do you live?"

"Don't worry about it."

The others girls looked at me as if I had overstepped, so Sabrina chimed in, pointing as she spoke. "She lives over there. I live around the corner, and Lillian, here"—she pointed at her, as if she couldn't speak for herself—"lives in the corner house over there." Sabrina moved closer to him as she spoke.

I was annoyed with her. I knew how boys' minds worked and understood that if we made them work for our information, they would like us more. But once Sabrina started there was no stopping her.

Oliver came down from their steps about the time that Sabrina was standing in front of their house. He looked at me and asked, "So what's your name?"

I was determined to stick to my game plan, so I smiled and said, "That's for me to know and for you to find out."

Oliver was about three years older than I, so when he laughed it was deep. I smiled, and he smiled back, but then I caught Chris looking at me too. He smiled, but his was raw. I couldn't look away, even when I wanted to.

Sabrina rolled her eyes and said, "That's Rebekah. She's the mysterious one."

I turned to her, annoyed and frustrated, and said, "Not so mysterious now, big mouth."

Sabrina was very beautiful, with thick black hair that fell past her waist. Boys fought over her, but she always made herself too available to them, so they quickly lost interest in her. She never knew her father. Her mother never spoke about him, so Sabrina would make up stories about him. He was either dead or taken by aliens, but either way he couldn't get to her, so he got a pass on his desertion of her and her sister. Boys became her outlet for the lack of male presence in her life. We all had similar stories, so we became a gang bonded by fatherlessness and overworked mothers. Our friendship with the boys came easily, and within days we became connected by lack and need.

Soon everyone noticed that Oliver was paying special attention to me. I pretended not to notice, but the girls were so jealous that they would constantly mention it. Sabrina was always first to speak. "You are so lucky. You should pay more attention to him." I would always roll my eyes at her. I couldn't explain to her that I had noticed him, but I also noticed his brother. Chris was always in trouble. He was a year younger than Oliver, and he was fearless. Girls fought over him no matter how much he lied to them and pitted them against each other. Some girls would talk about having sex with him as if that could keep him under control, but he always was the one in control. I knew all this about him, but when he looked at me, his look carried a shared secret I couldn't explain to anyone. I tried not to be alone with Chris. His raw sexuality caused me to feel things I didn't want to come alive. At fifteen, he was out of control, and I knew that he was only trouble, but my strange attraction to him kept me looking at him when no one could see me. His wickedness came from a place I understood.

When we would hang out in front of their home, we would occasionally catch his mother talking to Chris. He loved his mother. His eyes looked at her with an unquenchable desire that she never seemed to notice or appease. She would talk to him harshly and compare him to Oliver. She would call him a loser like his dad, wishing for the day he would grow up and leave. Oliver would listen and say nothing; actually, none of us would say anything. The shame that she poured on Chris splashed on all of us. We would stand with him, our heads down, feeling his defeat. Then she would move her gaze of disgust on all of us. Switching her tone, she would ask Oliver to come in and help her. "Yes, Mom," he'd say. And off he would go.

Sometimes my anger would rise toward Oliver, and my heart would break for Chris. I'd wonder why Oliver didn't stick up for his brother. In those moments, Oliver seemed cowardly, and I would stop talking to him for days. Chris would laugh it off, but I could see the pain in his eyes. I understood the loneliness behind them. Moments like those happened more frequently as we got closer. I never intended for anything more to happen between Chris and me, but as time went by, he began to change toward me. We noticed that he stayed away from us girls. When we were together, he became weird and awkward, fumbling for words and always looking down. So I was surprised when he showed up and caught me alone as I waited for Hector to come out of school. Standing in front of me, he said nothing at first. He noticed that I was uncomfortable.

I fidgeted until I was too irritated by his silent stare and asked, "What are you doing here?"

"You're different from the rest," he said.

I knew what he meant but pretended not to understand. "What are you talking about? You're crazy, Chris." I smiled, trying hard not to feel.

He got close to my face, and I could smell the beer on his breath. "You are different from the rest of the girls. Somehow, you know who I am and you don't try to change me."

"Move, Chris. I think you drank one too many beers." I tried to laugh, but he was getting too serious. I knew that Hector would be out soon and the girls would be coming around the corner.

"No, that's what you do. You move so that I can never catch you. Why do you move? What are you afraid of?"

Backing up, I said, "Look, Chris, I'm sorry about the way your mom treats you. I get it, but you need to do better. Not because of her but because of you. You know what I mean?"

He just looked at me and smiled. "That's why you're different because you see more than the rest. You try not to notice, but you do. It's hard for you to look away. That's good. That only means that you have a heart, a real heart. Don't give that up, Rebekah, or you may end up like me." He turned and walked away. My little brother came out the school door, but I didn't notice. I still was watching Chris. My heart broke for him.

Our little gang grew, which made it easier for me to keep away from Chris. Oliver showed up at my house almost every day after school. We would usually hang out in the front of my house or his. I did well in school, which kept my mother happy and away from me. I didn't want anything to interfere with my new life.

Outside, we played Motown music; the Jacksons kept us moving on cold winter days. Music and dancing became our form of entertainment. Lillian, a tall and lanky girl, would dance, and we would laugh at how little rhythm she had. Sabrina danced sexy, and when Chris was around, her hips moved especially slow. She wanted him, but he would never get near Sabrina. Sabrina also liked Oliver, but she knew that he was lost to me. On one of our evenings alone, Oliver asked me to go steady. I was young, and the thought made me laugh, but I still said yes. I liked Oliver, but I also had a strange attraction to his brother. I didn't understand my heart. It was going in two directions, and I couldn't control it, so I laughed to push it to the side.

Oliver was always kind and treated me as a gentleman would. Opening his heart was easy for him, and he offered it to me whenever he was around. But I had been broken into so many pieces that if anyone got close, I would cut, and Oliver got cut a lot. Whenever he would try to get too deep into my heart, telling me he loved me and that someday he wanted to take care of me, I would break it off with him and tell him that he was talking like a girl. I hated promises; especially ones that I knew were impossible. Oliver would stay away, but eventually he would come back to check on me. He knew that my mother was gone a lot, and he worried about my brother and me. I loathed the way I treated him. Eventually his kindness persuaded me to take him back.

Meanwhile, Chris also would come around, hoping that I would have a change of heart. He was dangerous, and I knew that if I chose him my life would never be the same. The direction of his life looked discouraging. Despite all I'd gone through, I still had remnants of hope given to me by the One who continued to rescue me.

My aunt came on occasion for the weekends. I had told her about my status in school, and she didn't want me to lose it. She was proud of the direction my life was going. She wanted to make sure it stayed that way, so she invested lots of money on clothing for me. My mother, trying her best, started buying me crazy socks, which became popular in school too. I was the girl with nice clothes and crazy socks. Everyone who met my aunt thought she was the coolest adult ever. Oliver had heard about her from everyone else. I didn't want to take a chance and introduce him to my family, so I never spoke of them. But one Saturday he decided to come by and meet her.

My aunt's eyes brightened at the sight of him, and she couldn't believe how cute he was. "Rebekah, he is so handsome, and he seems so nice." After meeting Oliver, she decided that I should have a birthday party. Once again she talked my mom into giving me a birthday party—and with no chaperones. My aunt helped buy most of the food. I invited everyone in my class and in our neighborhood. My aunt and mom put together a beautiful stream of balloons, crepe paper, and tulle in purple and fuchsia. Our apartment was very large—the dining room was joined to the living room that was joined to a sunroom. Everyone I invited came to my party, and it became the talk of the school—it was a smash.

That night I decided to love Oliver because my aunt loved him. After the party, we were inseparable. Chris came to the party with Sabrina. He laughed too loud and held Sabrina too close. I ignored him, but he kept staring at us all night. I felt sad for Sabrina and hoped she hadn't noticed his wandering eyes.

Oliver and I went steady for two months. I kept my distance from Chris, although I still would catch him looking at me. I felt drawn to him, but I knew it wasn't good.

Then it happened again, after I had dared to believe. "You have to go stay with your aunt," my mother said. "I have to move. I can't afford this place, and I need to get something smaller for now."

I felt as if someone was playing a cruel joke on me. I looked at her but said nothing. She walked away, leaving me alone in my room, looking for something to help me understand.

Oliver promised that he would always stay in touch. He wanted to marry me someday and promised that he would never stop loving me. I wanted desperately to believe him. Late one evening before I was to leave, Chris came to my bedroom window, which was located on the first floor. He began calling to me, asking me to come out. My room was near the back door, so I snuck out to meet him because I was worried that he would wake up my mother. I felt connected to him, and I wanted to leave with us being friends.

He was drunk and crying. "You are the only person I ever really liked. I was hoping that someday we would be together. I know my brother really likes you too, but he has my mother. I don't have anyone."

"Chris," I said, "a lot of girls like you."

"But none of them is you," he responded. The tears came down his face, and I couldn't resist. I hugged him. Without warning, he turned, and for a moment I got caught in his eyes. All my running had created a greater desire for him, one I hadn't realize until that moment. He kissed me and I let him. I sensed all that he was, good and bad, and knew that if I didn't leave, I'd get caught. I turned and ran back into my room.

"Rebekah, I'm sorry." I heard him choke on his tears as I ran. "I'm really going to miss you."

I left the next evening. Oliver hung out with me all day until it was time for me to go. He hugged me good-bye, and I felt like a traitor.

I waited for months for him to call, but it never came. I never saw either of them again. Today whenever the memory of them, of him, returns, I hope and pray that he, that they are happy.

CHAPTER 23

Making Sense of Senseless Never Makes Sense

A senseless man has no knowledge,
Nor does a stupid man understand this.
—Psalm 92:6

I was back at my aunt's for the summer. My thoughts of the home
I had left behind washed over me in waves of loneliness and pain.
I knew that things would never be the same, and that thought left
me weary. I cried all the time, even though my uncle tried to pacify
me. He tried to care for me and spoke in ways that made me believe
that he understood what I was going through.

"Baby girl, you're smart, and you have a lot of life to live. You're
a great singer and writer. Put all that you're feeling into that, and I
know you'll do great things. Don't stay stuck in your head. Let it
out." We bonded over politics, basketball (the Knicks, to be specific),
laughter, and food. But our greatest connection came through music.
I trusted him more than I trusted my aunt. She began to change
whenever I stayed with them, becoming impatient with me and
seeming to get on her husband's case all the time.

Every Saturday was cleaning day, and she took all day to clean the seven-hundred-square-foot apartment. Everything needed to be perfect, and nothing I did was ever enough. I was always assigned the bathroom, which was smaller than most closets. I was never taught how to clean or how she wanted it cleaned, but I was expected to know. She would yell at me, "You don't even know how to clean a bathroom. What is wrong with you?" Her words were curt and cut deep because she was my only source of faithful and steady hope.

Tony would tell her to stop and they would get into intense arguments. During their fights I would go outside to the stairwell. Their anger would drift out and find me. I wanted to disappear. After a few weeks of their constant back-and-forth, my aunt decided that I should stay with my mother and go to school there. She said they would pick me up on the weekends. My uncle reluctantly agreed, and I was once again shipped back to my mother's.

My mother had moved into a smaller apartment again. It reminded me of a train. Walking in through the back you would enter the kitchen. It was a very large room with a small bathroom in the corner. On the other end was a doorway that led to my mother's room, which connected to Hector's room, which connected to the living room. I hated that apartment. My mom tried to make it homey, but it was difficult when there was no privacy.

My mother had a new boyfriend. He had dark skin and straight dark hair. He was very handsome, and he knew it. He came in and out as if he owned the place, but he never helped with anything. My mom would complain about him, but whenever he showed up she would welcome him as if he were some kind of hero coming to save our lives. She would fuss over him, making him dinner and ignoring us to care for his needs. I started hating him. He and my mother argued all the time; my mother wanted more but he gave less. My mother would cry, asking him why he wouldn't commit to her, and he would respond that he wasn't ready. Yet he was always ready to come over and pretend to be the man of the house. He would tell my mom and brother what to do, but when it came to me, he would back off. Whenever he tried to say something to me, I would stare at him as if he were something that had just fallen off my shoe.

I left on the weekends, which meant he stayed with my mother. By the time I returned on Sunday evenings, he would be gone. The longer he stayed with my mother, the more abusive he became. He called my mother unspeakable names. I could feel my anger rising toward him and her. I didn't understand why my mother was staying with a person who treated her with such disrespect. My frustration about the situation came out, and once again I began speaking to her belligerently. I was losing any respect for her. It was during this time that my greatest heartbreak came.

As my aunt had suggested, I spent weekends with her and my uncle. I loved my time with them, especially with my uncle. In my mind, he became the father I didn't have. He would tell me stories of his childhood in Puerto Rico and that his father was the most important man in his life. He told the worst jokes, but I laughed because I wanted to show him that I loved him. Sometimes I would catch him staring at me, and I knew that he loved me too. I needed him to love me, so I let every defense down in order to feel the fullness of his love. During this time my aunt looked unhappy. It came out in the way she spoke. It didn't matter what we were doing, she would blame me, complain about me, or simply call me unkind names. I loved my aunt. I didn't understand her bitterness toward me. I could see that at times my aunt felt bad for the way she had treated me, so she would make my favorite foods.

During our last winter weekend together, my uncle and I made snow angels and had a massive snowball fight. My aunt watched from the window and waved whenever I looked at her. I wished she would join us, but she never wanted to. It was Sunday, so my uncle had to take me home that evening. My aunt decided to stay home, telling us that she was tired.

He and I drove off alone in the car we had named Blue Eyes, a blue Datsun hatchback. The drive from New York to New Jersey was about one hour long. He played music, and I listened and sang along. Thirty minutes into the drive, he turned off the music. I turned toward him and caught him smiling at me. I smiled back, happy for our time together. I was holding a container full of fruit my aunt had made for me, another peace offering for words harshly spoken that weekend. I don't know why I kept looking at the container as he spoke, but I couldn't take my eyes off of it.

He started by saying, "Baby girl, I have to tell you something, but I don't want you to tell your *titi*. I know that you're only fourteen, but you are a woman now. Did you know that women in Puerto Rico marry at the age of fourteen?" I couldn't look at him. Something about the way he was talking changed the atmosphere in the car and kept me focused on my aunt's container of fruit. "I want you to know that if you don't want to, I won't, but I want you. I'm in love with you the way a man loves a woman, and I want to be with you that way. Do you understand, baby girl?" I couldn't respond, so I sat staring at the stupid container. "I know you love your titi, but she doesn't have to know. We can keep it a secret. Think about it, okay? We can talk more when you come back." He touched my hand. I wanted to leave. I wanted to die. I wanted to go back to the way things were.

When he dropped me off, he leaned down and kissed me gently on the lips, saying, "Don't worry. She won't know our secret, okay? Love you, baby girl. Be good." He went around and opened the door for me and walked me to my mother's apartment.

My mother opened the door and I walked straight through the caboose into the living room, holding the container as if my life depended on it. I wanted to be as far away from my uncle as possible. I sat in the darkness, praying that God would send someone to rescue me. I knew that I couldn't tell my mother. I sat alone and cried. Maybe this is where I got the crazy idea that my real father would finally rescue me. Senseless moments lend themselves to senseless thoughts. Too bad no one was there to bring me back to sense.

That same Sunday evening my mom's boyfriend decided to stay over. Most times he would leave as soon as I arrived, but I returned late that night, and he was feeling bold. I could hear them in the next room. I couldn't sleep. I heard their voices getting louder as he threatened her. She screamed, and I heard the familiar sound of fist hitting flesh. *Thump, thump, thump.* The sound ignited something I had never felt. I got out of my bed and headed for the kitchen. I had to go through their room, and I saw him sitting on top of my mom, hitting her in the face. I walked into the kitchen and grabbed the biggest knife I could find. I went back into their room, stepped on the bed, grabbed the man by the hair with my left hand, pulled back, and put the knife to his throat.

He didn't expect me, so when I started talking to him, he tried to get loose. As I pressed the knife against his neck, I said, "If you move, I will kill you. I don't care what happens to you, so you better just get up and leave, and don't come back because I will kill you."

He didn't move a muscle. He simply told my mom, "Do something. Tell her to get the knife off my neck before she kills me." When she didn't respond, he started begging my mom.

But she had had enough. "You better do what she says" was all she had to say.

As he moved, I pressed the knife against his back. He started cursing me in Spanish, but I didn't care. I wanted him to do something stupid. We walked back through the kitchen, and as he open the door, I kicked him in the rear and cursed at him. I locked the door behind him and heard him bang the door with his fist before he walked away.

I threw the knife in the sink on my way to my room, and it clamored against the metal sink in protest at my disrespect of its protection. I'd wanted to kill him and hurt him in the way that I was hurting—and the feeling frightened me.

He eventually came back, but he never spoke to me. I noticed that he had a small scar where the knife had nicked him. He never tried to hit my mother again, and eventually he faded away. I was happy to see him go.

I didn't know what to do about my uncle. I stopped going to their home, which meant spending more time at my mother's home. I hated being there. My mother was going through a depression over losing her boyfriend, and she became impossible to be around. I hated her weakness and her weeping and complaining about the lack of good men. I started staying out more and found other kids my age to hang with.

My uncle wouldn't stop calling me. He wanted to make sure that I hadn't told anyone, and I hadn't. My mother was in an agitated state. I was beyond understanding her. I decided to call my father. I wanted to go back and live with him and especially my brothers.

I had to call several times, but I finally got him. I told him what had transpired between Tony and me and asked him if he would pick me up. He was silent for a moment and then said he would call me back. I waited for what seemed like forever, but within days of my calling my dad, my aunt called me. Her voice was cold and lifeless, and I instantly knew that my father had spoken to her.

"We're picking you up in two Saturdays from today, so be ready. No excuses. We're going to Lancaster to fix this mess you created. After all that I've done for you, this is how you repay me. You're unbelievable." And with that she hung up the phone. She never asked me if it was true.

That was Tuesday. By the end of the week, I tried to commit suicide again. First, I tried to jump off a high bridge but was stopped by kids in the neighborhood. Then I went into the bathroom with a knife. The kids had told my mother my intention, and she banged on the bathroom door, trying to get me out. My mom called the police, and when they arrived I pulled the knife on the police, so they sprayed mace in my face.

My aunt and uncle picked me up early the following Saturday. We didn't say a word to each other. I sat in the back of Blue Eyes and wished I could die. Be careful what you wish for because it might happen. I didn't know this bit of wisdom then, but I don't think it would've stopped what came next.

CHAPTER 24

Oh Death, Where Art Thou?

The cords of death entangled me, and the
anguish of the grave came over me.
—Psalms 116: 3

Death comes in many forms, so when it came for me, I didn't know its face. I thought I was trying to protect myself, but numbness created for emotional protection killed everything in me. Even places I never meant to sacrifice.

We sat on the playground at Martin Luther King School. My aunt, uncle, and dad sat at least twenty feet away, but their faces seemed pronounced in the brightness of the day. Their lips held perpetual smiles that made them look anxious and silly. My aunt kept rocking back and forth, as if the motion could soften the ground beneath her. My uncle smiled, but it didn't reach his eyes, which was unusual for him. Every once in a while my aunt shot a look at me that said I had a terminal disease, and they were going to treat it. While speaking, she contorted her face to show disgust or rolled her eyes, belittling whoever she was talking about. My father had his back turned to me, which felt natural and evoked little feeling on my behalf. Instead, I focused on my uncle, but he never looked at me.

On our way to Lancaster, he only spoke to my aunt, who looked pleased to have all of his attention. She smiled at him and reached out to touch him, as if he needed consoling. They created a space that no longer involved me. They were in alliance against me, and it brought them closer than I had ever seen them. Looking at her sitting in the same seat where I'd been sitting when he had proclaimed his love for me made me feel sorrowful for her. Didn't she know how foolish she looked, believing his lies? There were times when my aunt would look away, and I would catch him looking at me through the rearview mirror. His eyes that once held love and concern now held contempt and anger. I had betrayed him again. This time there was no going back. I couldn't hold his gaze for long, so I always looked away first. I wasn't surprised that now, on the playground, he wouldn't look at me. His message had come through loud and clear in the car. The love that he once had for me had turned to hate, and the sight of me made him angry.

They spoke for about an hour. Walking back toward me, they looked at me as if they were ready to do battle, three against me. My dad took the first swipe, berating me and accusing me of lying. My aunt followed up with accusations of my lack of appreciation. She couldn't believe that I would tell such lies after all that she and her husband had done for me. That began the barrage of accusations, as my father and aunt took turns stepping on me. I wished that my father would show me mercy and hit me. I looked at his belt and prayed that he would use it, but they kept talking, and the impact of each word was worse than any beating I had ever received. My uncle stood behind them, watching me. I looked at him while they spoke, hoping that the love he once had for me would step in and save me, saying, "Hey, wait a minute. Sorry, everyone, but I did say those things to her. Sorry. I was out of my mind. I was just joking with her, and I forgot to tell her."

But he didn't say anything. They kept asking me why I had lied but how could I respond when the truth wasn't what they wanted to hear? Finally, when they saw that I wasn't going to reply, they stepped away, shaking their heads in disapproval.

As soon as they walked away, I lay down on the grass. It was a beautiful cool day. The sun was bright and a light breeze fanned gently across my face. I knew that if I wanted to, I could open my eyes and Jesus would be near, but once again I wanted nothing to do with His goodness. I concluded that I was evil and therefore incapable of deserving good. I had heard it said enough at my uncle's church—bad things happen to those who aren't good enough for God. I no longer felt like His favorite. I had forgotten our times together. I gave Him up and allowed evil to come. I lay back and closed my eyes. I didn't want to look at the sun or feel the breeze. I lay down deep into my brokenness and allowed the shadows to come to me, and one by one, they did. I felt their fist beat me and with each blow something new started to change me. I realized how long I had been fighting the feeling. Giving up now felt natural and necessary.

Numbness entered first. It allowed everything that came after to settle into the crevices of my soul. Fissures that had developed during my years of pain opened up like dried desert cracks and soaked in everything that came next. Worthlessness, shame, anger, hate, self-loathing, and abandonment came down in torrents that beat into me with such severity that I felt bruises well up on my flesh. I curled my body, but the beatings came down harder, and the bruises began taking root, going deep into places I had thought were locked safely.

Then I felt her. Little Girl Me called out for help from somewhere deep inside. She wanted to live. She wanted someone to love her. But I was done with her. As my tears began to flow, I vowed I would never feel this way again. I hated Little Girl Me because of all she wanted. She was foolish to believe that anyone could love such a mess, so I called them to kill her. I wanted that emotional, hope-filled, heartfelt girl to die, so I asked everything dark that was beating into me to kill her. With each onslaught came another truth of who I wasn't.

I wasn't loved. I wasn't cared for. I wasn't wanted. I wasn't good. I wasn't, I wasn't, I wasn't … I heard her crying. She tried to stop me, but numbness had done its job. I didn't feel anything. I wanted all that was good in me gone.

When I woke up, I was in my bed at my mother's house. As I opened my eyes, my mother came and sat on my bed and asked if I was doing okay. She said that I had been sick with a fever since returning from Lancaster. She said that I hadn't spoken since my return and wondered if I wanted to talk. I shook my head and asked her to leave me alone. She got up and walked away but turned around before leaving and said, "Your titi is right about you. You are very ungrateful." One final blow before finally dying. With that, my mother left the room, and I went down into a deep hole where Little Girl Me was now buried and dead, and I was glad to see her go.

CHAPTER 25

Before We Rise, We First Must Reach

For I am the Lord, your God who
takes hold of your right hand
And says to you, do not fear; I will help you.
—Isaiah 41:13

For the next three years I went from house to house. No one wanted a stinky corpse living in their home. After returning from Lancaster, I lived with my mom for a couple of months. I became rebellious and talked back to her all the time. I reminded her of how worthless a mother she was and told her that I wished she really was dead. I told her that no one would ever love her and that she looked foolish trying so hard to be loved. After a few months, she had had enough and asked my aunt to take me.

My aunt reluctantly agreed, but our relationship had deteriorated. I hurt around her and did everything in my power to annoy her, including not picking up after myself, not cleaning the bathroom when she asked, and talking ugly to her. At times she tried to love me as best she could, even giving me a small Sweet Sixteen party, but I was in a place too dark for small fragments of love. My uncle Tony completely checked out. He never got in between us again and spoke very little to me, and at times he would completely leave the apartment. When I lived with them, my presence caused a chasm between them. It was difficult for my aunt because she couldn't handle her husband or me. So sending me back to my father's house was always the only solution.

Back in my father's house, I began to talk back to Diana and ignore my father. The house was still in a state of chaos, but it made me feel welcomed. I began to act chaotic, and Diana complained about me incessantly. Although her complaints were valid at times, my new fearlessness didn't care about fairness. My father told Diana to shut up and leave him alone. He didn't want to deal with me anymore. He was getting tired of everyone coming to him to fix me.

Then he couldn't take it anymore. I was called into the boys' room, where they all stood, watching me enter. Diana stood next to my father, as happy as a cat with a bird in its mouth. My father turned to each of my brothers and told them to apologize to her. The why was lost on me since I wasn't privy to the first part of their meeting. My brothers put their heads down, and John said, "Sorry, Mom." Then Josiah said, "Sorry, Mom." All eyes fell on me as my turn loomed over me. I had stopped calling this woman Mom weeks ago, but I knew if I didn't say the words exactly as my brothers had, my father would lose it. I looked at them looking at me and then turned to my father and stared at him.

My father's eyes widened with disbelief, and he yelled, "You better apologize and call her Mom when you say it, or I'm going to beat the evil out of you."

I could see that my brothers were visibly shaking. Then I looked at Diana. She stood looking at me as if she had won; As if the bird she was chewing on would give up without flapping a wing. So I flapped. "I'm not saying sorry to her for anything. I didn't do anything, and she's not my mother, so I'm not going to call her Mom. Go ahead and beat it out of me!"—by this time I was screaming—"I don't care anymore! Go ahead and kill me!"

His eyes became wild. He yelled curses at me. He grabbed me by the hair. As he yanked me out of the room, I took a quick look at Diana, and her face looked dejected. Then I caught her looking at me, and I smiled.

My father dragged me into my room. He began beating me with his fist like a man. Shouting with every ounce of volume I had, I began to scream, "Kill me! Kill me! Kill me!"

"Cry!" Fist to face. "Cry!" Fist to face. "Cry!" my father yelled as he beat me. But I wouldn't cry. I felt nothing, no matter how hard he hit me. Then he picked up a wooden lamp from my side table, a heavy lamp that James had made in wood shop. My father beat my body with it, but all I did was scream, "Kill me!" In the madness of the moment, he lost his mind and had lifted the lamp to bash me in the head when Josiah jumped on top of me. The lamp hit his back, and I heard the air being knocked out of him. I begged him to get off. The bottom of the lamp had broken, and my father was back to punching and trying to pull my brother off.

Then through all the craziness, Josiah leaned into my ear and whispered, "Rebekah, please cry." I could hear each thump against his back as he was being beaten and felt the warmth of his tears against my cheek, and I knew it was my fault. At that moment a small measure of emotion came through, and tears came down my face for my brother.

My father finally pulled him off, and when he saw me crying, he walked away. My brother collapsed next to me on the bed. He was hurting and could barely move. I closed my eyes and was saddened by the fact that I was still alive and breathing in painful bursts of air.

Weeks later, I was sent away again. During this time I had learned how to go away for weeks at a time. I walked around and could respond to whatever was being said, but I was devoid of emotion. At night I lay on a couch or makeshift bed and heard adults discussing how quickly they could get rid of me. I would turn over and fall asleep with dreams of demons beating and mocking me, but my numbness reached inside my dreams, and I felt nothing.

Then the ability for me to leave was taken. I was walking to school and could feel myself leaving when an audible voice said to me, "If you leave again, you will never come back." The voice caused great fear to rise in me. I didn't understand why, but I knew I couldn't leave anymore. I stayed awake after that encounter, but it only produced more anger and disillusionment in me. I clung to my numbness like a child holding on to her filthy security blanket.

I don't remember all the people I stayed with during those three years of death, but by the time I came back to my father's home, I felt desperate. No one could control me, and no one wanted to deal with me. I returned to my father's, but I was so dead that I was cutting myself more often and deeper. I was desperate to feel something— anything other than the deep numbness that had cemented itself into my spirit. I couldn't cry. It felt as if everything inside me had completely dried up. Sitting in church, I would watch as others cried and sometimes broke down uncontrollably. I watched their faces and wondered what could produce such enormous waves of emotion.

One Sunday, the Holy Spirit moved in such a way that people came to the front weeping. I looked at them and thought, *I want to feel that.* I closed my eyes, but no matter how hard I tried, I felt nothing.

Days later, as my brothers and I walked the three miles to school, I started talking to Jesus. It had been a while since I had spoken to him. Somewhere along the way I had lost touch, but as soon as I started talking to Him, I felt a familiar rush come to my spirit. I called out to Him for a whole week. I kept telling Him, "Help me to cry; help me to feel." I wanted my heart to come back to life, but I didn't realize that I would need profound heart surgery. A week and two days later, He began my surgery, one that would begin a lifetime of surgeries, one great procedure at a time.

CHAPTER 26

There's Life after Death after Life

See, I set before you today life and
prosperity, death and destruction.
—Deuteronomy 30:15

It was Tuesday, which is probably the most blah day of the week. I enjoyed the peace that I received walking to and from school, and today was no different. School had been uneventful. My thoughts were mulling over homework that needed to be done. Hearing His voice wasn't in my thoughts. I had forgotten the SOS I had sent out the week before, but Jesus never forgets. He waited until I was standing in front of my house before He spoke: "Go to church." I knew what He meant. We went to my uncle's church, and that was the only place I would have gone. My feet were tired, and I really wanted to drop off my books, but the voice sounded determined.

I ran inside, laid my books down, and immediately ran out, heading toward the church. Then I remembered that the church would be closed. I told the voice within me, "It's closed right now." I didn't hear a response. I was desperate, so I continued to walk the two miles toward the church. I believed that the same spirit that had directed me to go would find a way to get me inside. When I got to the glass doors I could see that no one was inside. I reached for the doors and without hesitation pulled them open. I walked into the large lobby that was filled with dark shadows, diluted by the light coming in from a picture window that faced three crosses. I sensed that the battle had already begun. I felt fear grip me, and for a moment I wanted to turn and run away. What was I doing in such a dark place alone? But my heart's need for Him was greater than the fear.

Without thought, I walked toward the gold handles of the sanctuary doors and pulled them open. Immediately I was welcomed by streams of green light that flowed from ten-foot windows. There were eight light green tinted windows that flanked the sides of the sanctuary. As I walked down the aisle, I saw them. Standing in front of each window was a warrior angel that stood at least twenty feet tall and was ready for battle. They never looked or moved, but their presence overpowered my fear. Gone was the anxiety I felt when I'd seen the shadows in the lobby. As I walked down the aisle, I noticed that the green light was reflecting off their armor and beating back the dark shadows that had made their way from the lobby to the corners of the altar. The angels' presence imparted peace, and I sensed their fierce protection over me. I knew He had sent them for me. But why would He?

My uncle's church was large enough to seat over a thousand people, but it grew larger as I walked down the aisle. The altar felt farther away than my previous two miles, and I could feel my legs trembling at the presence of heaven and hell in one place. By the time I got to the altar, my feet ached, but the ache in my heart was worse. The things in the corner couldn't touch me, but their words filtered through the darkness into my ears. They spoke of my shame and worthlessness. When one dared to reach for me, the light from an angel's sword sliced though the darkness. It squealed in pain as it retreated back into darkness.

As I reached the altar, I went to my right and kneeled down in the corner. As my knees touched the floor, I felt myself being elevated outside my body. I could see myself encased in green light, but I wasn't in the church anymore. I was taken into my past hurts, one by one. I saw myself at two, being slapped and taken to a crib. There was Jesus, standing next to the crib. I was taken back to my mother's bloody body as she lay on the bathroom floor. There He was with His hand on my head, weeping for both my mother and me.

Then something in me filled with fear as He took me back into the dark alley. Talons of hopelessness gripped my heart. I put my hand on my chest, afraid that it would rip open and expose all that I had hidden. The boys' laughter was loud as I felt myself drowning. For a few moments I couldn't breathe. I believed I would die. Then, from the corner of my eye came a light that cut through the darkness. My fear lay exposed. It looked no greater than the Wizard of Oz behind the great dark curtain. But truth can only heal if it's believed and I was not capable of believing yet. Abandonment, abuse, shame, and worthlessness were fighting to keep me. Even after seeing the reality of all that He was showing me, I couldn't free myself from them. Yet He never gave up and continued to take me to painful places. In each place, whenever I looked around, I saw Him standing near. I never saw myself alone, even when in my natural state I was.

There were times I would see myself pushing Him, but He was never farther than an arm's length away. Sometimes He smiled; other times He wept. Then I saw myself at Martin Luther King Park and watched as a great cloud covered me, encasing me in a dark cocoon. Even in this state, He never left my side. At times, things like arms would reach out of the cocoon to push Him away, but they would always retreat in fear. His eyes never left me.

These visions took me to deeper places of pain and hurt, as I saw the grief I had unleashed on my mother, my aunt, my abuela, and even Diana. A part of me wanted Him to stop. Dark forces fought for me to open my eyes and run out of the church, but I wasn't ready to leave Him. My heart knew I needed Him or an important part of me would die forever. Then He took me to the edge of what was once beautiful but now seemed too lost to restore. I wept in fear, knowing that what He was about to show me would be the most frightening vision of all.

We were back in our secret place, our garden. There, I stood alone with Him. The flowers that once greeted me were gone and so was the brightness of His light. We were surrounded by dullness, as if a great cloud was trying to snuff out the beauty of His light. Then, as I looked beyond Him, I saw the perpetrator. There before me was a great wall that went as high as my eyes could see and as wide. It was made of brick and mortar. Each brick held words etched into them with childlike writing. As I got closer I realized that it was the wall that I had been building for most of my young life. Looking around me, I saw the stream that once flowed with rubies, emeralds, and diamonds, and I realized that it had stopped flowing. Gone was the life that created such splendor, and in its place was a dark, dry hole, surrounded by crusty dirt. I could see that something or someone had disturbed a small patch of dirt, but I wasn't ready to look.

I stared at the great wall and wondered how I ever could bring it down. Its size was daunting, and all the words of shame gave the wall power that felt perverted in what was once a beautiful garden. Flowers no longer grew, and the ground was full of weeds and dead things. Standing next to the hole, Jesus waited patiently as I looked around at all that I had created. I looked down and saw that His feet were dirty. For whatever reason, this made me cry. Why would he come back to a place that I had destroyed?

Then I looked at what He had been looking at, and my heart seized. As I looked at a pile of dirt, I saw the edges of a once beautiful pink tulle of Little Girl Me. I fell to my knees and asked Him to forgive me. I mourned and wailed bitterly for Little Girl Me. I had killed and buried her in the very place where she once had found life. Each tear fell onto ground that was parched and cracked. I couldn't stop weeping at what I had done. Feelings of love began to flow like shock waves, and I couldn't control the shaking in my body.

I came back to my uncle's church, still kneeling in the corner. It was Tuesday. It was youth night, and I wasn't alone anymore. There was a sea of people, weeping with mouths wide open. As I stood, I couldn't walk freely because everyone was tightly knit together, body to body. I marveled at the sight and wondered what had happened.

Later, I was told that people coming in had heard me crying. I was so loud that they became concerned and came to console me. As soon as they touched me, they fell to their knees and began weeping too. Meanwhile, other people kept coming in, and as soon as they touched or neared another person who was weeping, they would fall to their knees and begin weeping. The front of the church was full of people and they spilled down the aisle. Some were kneeling while others lay flat on their backs or on their faces, but they all were crying, some mixed with laughter and others in deep sorrow. Service was unable to start. Everyone who entered became consumed with what God was doing.

All the tears cried that night began to fill the once-dried stream. Little Girl Me began to rise that night, but the fight wasn't over. I had to remove each brick from my vast wall, one piece at a time, but He told me a secret: "Start at the bottom."

It's wondrous to watch enormous portions of my wall come crumbling down, allowing His great light access into my once dark and dead places.

Epilogue

I wish I could tell you that my life had a happy ending, but fairy tales are restricted to those things that have no life; God is all about life, and life is never easy. My life journey has been a very difficult one. I never forgot my relationship with Him, but I have walked away from our path many times. Thank goodness He has never let me wander too far. It's taken a lifetime of hurts and healing to bring me to this place where I have learned that I could trust Him with every part of my life—not an easy thing to do when what God requires is always bigger than we are able to understand. Whenever I go back to the garden, I weep. This is where my first true love began, and with every visit I find myself deeper in love with Him.

As children we all have experienced a secret place where we felt safe; a place where our child spirit would go to get away from those things that seemed harsh and out of our control. I know that many of you may feel that you have lost your way to that place. Life's hurts and mistakes may make you feel that you have wandered too far, and going back may seem like a cruel dream. But what if the truth were an arm's length away, and all you had to do was reach?

I sincerely believe that Jesus is waiting for you to reach and believe as children believe. No preconceived notions or displaced ideas of what offering is needed to bring before Him. He can render

His redemption without any sacrifice because Jesus has done that for us. He simply wants you to come back into your secret place with Him. There, He will show you things that only He can heal and resurrect. It will not be easy, but in your weakness you will be strong in Him, who created you and knows you intimately.